Back to *Basics*

Fundamentals of
Sharpening

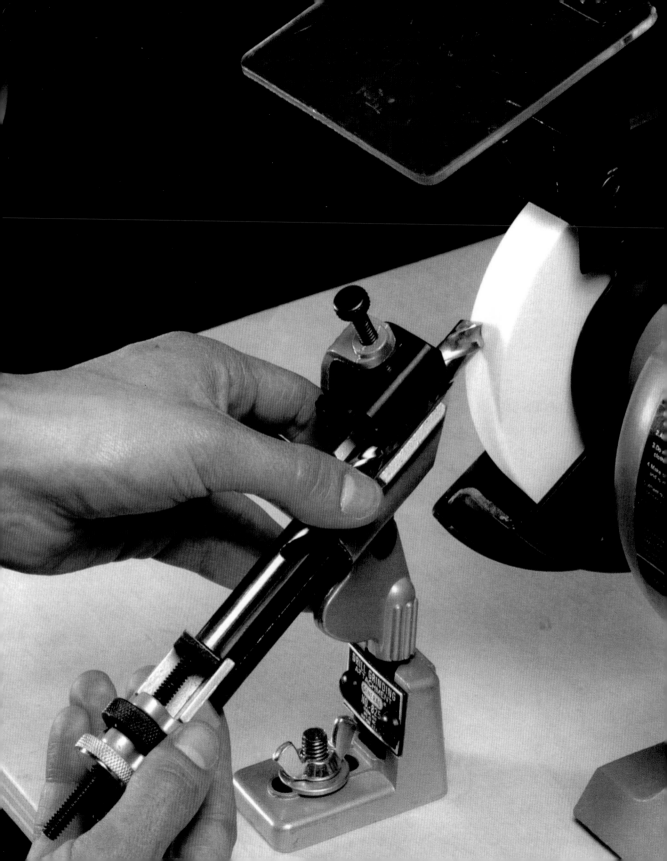

Back to Basics

Fundamentals of
Sharpening

Straight Talk for Today's **Woodworker**

skills institute
press

Distributed By
Fox Chapel Publishing

FOX CHAPEL
PUBLISHING

© 2010 by Skills Institute Press LLC
"Back to Basics" series trademark of Skills Institute Press
Published and distributed in North America by Fox Chapel Publishing Company, Inc.

Fundamentals of Sharpening is an original work, first published in 2010.

Portions of text and art previously published by and reproduced under license with Direct Holdings Americas Inc.

ISBN 978-1-56523-496-3

Library of Congress Cataloging-in-Publication Data
Fundamentals of sharpening.
   p. cm. -- (Back to basics)
Includes index.
ISBN 978-1-56523-496-3
1. Woodworking tools. 2. Sharpening of tools.
TT186.F86 2010
684'.082--dc22

               2010004521

To learn more about the other great books from Fox Chapel Publishing, or to find a retailer near you, call toll-free 800-457-9112 or visit us at *www.FoxChapelPublishing.com*.

Note to Authors: We are always looking for talented authors to write new books in our area of woodworking, design, and related crafts. Please send a brief letter describing your idea to Acquisition Editor, 1970 Broad Street, East Petersburg, PA 17520.

Printed in China
First printing: October 2010

Contents

Introduction 8

Chapter 1: Sharpening Basics .12

Chapter 2: Maintaining Hand Tools 24

Chapter 3: Sharpening Blades and Bits 58

Chapter 4: Carving Tools 86

Index 116

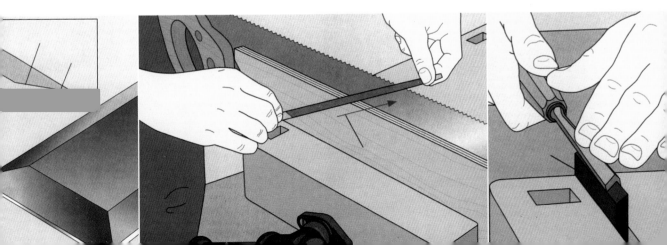

What You Can Learn

Sharpening Basics, p. 12

Regular attention to tool condition will speed, rather than retard, progress and improve both the quality of work and enjoyment of it.

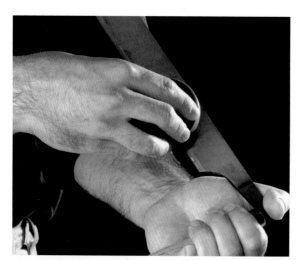

Maintaining Hand Tools, p. 24

Handsaws, chisels, and planes play a vital role in many cabinetmaking tasks, from cutting joints and chopping mortises to smoothing stock.

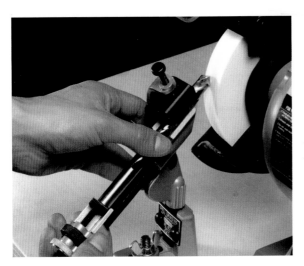

Sharpening Blades and Bits, p. 58

A dull drill bit will tend to skate off a workpiece rather than biting cleanly into the wood.

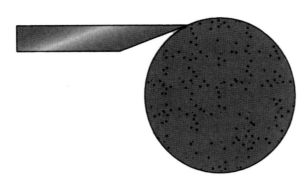

Carving Tools, p. 86

This section demonstrates the sharpening techniques you will need to practice the craft of carving.

Value of Sharp Tools

When I was a kid I thought working wood was really difficult. It was, too, because my dad's tool bench was dominated by rough screwdrivers and assorted wrenches, dull saws, and a few auger bits. I remember it with fondness because it helped set me on my life's path, but it sure didn't encourage me to master the pieces of rough, splitty pine that I occasionally worked on.

Sharp hand tools were a revelation to a guy who grew up thinking that woodworking required some sort of special genius and a lot of powerful equipment. When I encountered a craftsman who built fine country furniture, miles from the nearest power line, I was inspired to learn as much as I could about how to make tools work well. As a result, wood became a much more welcoming material to me. Today, as a seasoned teacher of woodworking to children, my job is to help my students appreciate the possibilities of wood. The last thing I want to do is let them work with bum tools.

It is easy to fall in love with hand tools. I have a small collection of time-mellowed implements that I would not think of putting to work. They represent a history of effort and problem-solving that is a comfort to my modern mind. I also have other fine old tools that are frequently put into service. But the tools I use every day in teaching have much less of an aura about them. Kids bang them around and drop them all too frequently. What is important about them is that they work right.

The difference between a dull tool and a sharp one is something every woodworker needs to know. It is the difference between the frustrated kid I was and the kids I teach today. When I show a child how to whittle, he or she is expected to try every knife on the rack, usually four or five tools. Only by making this comparison will it become clear which are really sharp and which are just okay.

Every woodworker has his or her own preferred way to sharpen an edge tool. Some use oil stones, slow sandstone wheels, Arkansas stones, or leather strops. Others prefer Japanese water stones, the use of which is almost a ritual. In my school shop, I need to work quickly and I have long since settled on a grinding belt and buffing wheel. At home, I have fallen in love with the new technology of diamond stones.

I firmly believe that, while sharp tools are essential, there is no one right way to sharpen tools, only the best way for you. It takes time to figure it out, but it is time you must be willing to spend. It is like building the foundation of your home. Everything else rests on it.

- Richard Starr

Richard Starr has taught woodworking to middle school students in Hanover, New Hampshire, since 1972. His book *Woodworking with Kids* is published by Taunton Press. Starr has written numerous articles for *Fine Woodworking*, *Today's Woodworker*, and other publications. His television series *Woodworking for Everyone* was broadcast on public television.

Different Ways to Sharpen

The old adage "Tools do not make the craftsman" contains a degree of truth. Still, sharp tools—although they will not make you a craftsperson—will greatly improve and enhance your skills. In fact, in my opinion, a great deal of skill displayed by today's craftspeople is based largely on their ability to create and maintain a keen edge on their cutting tools.

My wood turning travels throughout North America, Australia, and New Zealand have brought me in contact with many first-class woodworkers, carvers, wood turners, and just plain "hewers" of wood. They have worked in schools, home workshops, and craft fairs, with a variety of tools from the very best high-speed steel to the crudest homemade implements. Still, they all had one thing in common: They used sharp tools.

As varied as the crafts and craftspeople are, so are their methods and tools used for sharpening. Each one, used correctly, will create a keen cutting edge. The best are those that do not overheat cutting edges. This is probably the most common problem experienced by novices when sharpening tools. It is especially serious if the tool is made of carbon tool steel rather than high-speed steel. When carbon tool steel is heated until it turns blue the "temper" or "hardness" is removed, and the tool becomes soft and will not hold an edge for more than a few seconds. High-speed steel, on the other hand, will sustain a great deal of heat without damage.

The simple solution to "tip burning" is to use sharpening equipment that does not generate high heat or to use equipment that is constantly cooling the cutting edge as it is being ground. Wet grinding will assure the woodworker a cool cutting edge for two reasons: First, the grinding wheel is flooded with a coolant (usually water) to prevent heat buildup and second, the wet grinding wheels usually turn at a very slow rate which reduces the heat generated by the grinding process. Personally, I find the wet grinding system both too slow and too messy. My experience with wet grinding has been one of constantly cleaning the slurry of sawdust and water from the stone.

My preference for sharpening is a white aluminum oxide grinding wheel followed by a quick touch-up on an extra-fine neoprene honing wheel. I choose the aluminum oxide wheel simply because its porosity makes it a very cool grinding wheel compared to old gray stone or the standard sanding belts or discs. It is also very fast-cutting, thereby reducing the time at the grinder and reducing the time allowed for the heat to build up on the cutting edge. To hone my tools I use a neoprene wheel because it is fast and it maintains the hollow grind formed by the grinding wheel.

- Ian Waymark

Ian Waymark has taught industrial education in Canada for 16 years. He is the owner of Woodturner's World, a store on Gabriola Island, British Columbia, that specializes in wood turning tools. Waymark designed the Orca 1 lathe and the Sabre Sharpening Center.

Sharpening Basics

At one time or another, virtually every woodworker has looked upon tool sharpening as a rainy-day task, an onerous duty undertaken only as a last resort that seems calculated to delay progress on the moment's favorite project. Although it may be impossible to persuade all woodworkers to embrace the joys of tool sharpening—as some do—sooner or later, most adopt an attitude of enlightened self interest, an understanding that regular attention to tool condition will speed, rather than retard, progress and improve both the quality of work and enjoyment of it.

In Japan, apprentice woodworkers spend years at the sharpening bench before attempting to cut wood. The practice is rooted in reality: To cut and finish wood, one must use sharp tools.

The most realistic route to sharp tools for most woodworkers lies in regular attention. When sharpening and maintenance are adopted as part of regular workshop routine, the time required is reduced—and the benefits of keen edges are quickly realized.

There are many jigs and accessories that promise quick and easy results, and no shortage of techniques with the same goal. But all sharpening work comes down to this: Tools are sharpened by wearing away steel to form a fine edge, and polishing that edge so it slices as accurately and effortlessly as

possible. Among many tools, two are essential: a sharpening stone and a grinder.

Once, all sharpening stones came from the ground; sandstone, novaculite, and other materials have been quarried and cut into bench stones (*page 18*) from the earliest days of woodworking. More recently, technology has produced synthetic stones that substitute for the dwindling supply of natural abrasives.

A somewhat older technology also provided the foot-powered sandstone grinding wheel and its descendant, the bench grinder (*page 20*), which saves much labor in removing nicks and forming bevels before final honing.

This chapter is intended to remove the mystery and some of the labor from the sharpening process. With a grinder, a few benchstones, an understanding of the process (*page 14*), and practice, you can have sharper tools—and derive more pleasure from your woodworking.

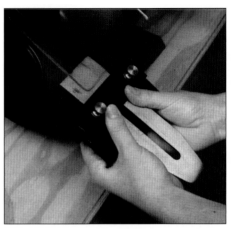

The nicked cutting edge of a plane blade is squared on a bench grinder. Clamping the blade in a commercial grinding jig keeps the end of the blade perpendicular to the grinder's abrasive wheel.

A Japanese finish stone is being used to polish the back of a butt chisel.

The Cutting Edge

A cutting edge can be defined as two flat, polished surfaces meeting at an angle. Since most blades are designed to be pushed through wood, a keen cutting edge is essential, particularly for dense hardwoods that can quickly blunt tools. Any flaw, like a nick in a planer knife or a chisel blade, will be transferred to the wood being cut.

Do not assume that just because a chisel is new that its edge is as sharp or as straight as it should be. Even the best steel is likely to show manufacturing imperfections. Low-quality tools, however, may never achieve and hold an edge.

In its simplest form, sharpening is like sanding: It consists of the wearing away of one material by a harder material, using successively finer abrasives. When the bevel of a chisel is drawn across a sharpening stone, the abrasive particles scratch the surface of the chisel uniformly, creating a flat surface.

The difference between a dull and sharp cutting edge becomes obvious when a blade cuts into wood. On the left-hand side of the wood surface shown above, a well-sharpened chisel severed the wood fibers cleanly, producing thin shavings; a dull chisel tore the wood fibers on the right-hand side of the board. Another way to determine whether a blade is sharp or dull is to examine the cutting edge itself, a dull edge reflects more light than a sharp one.

How Sharp is Sharp?

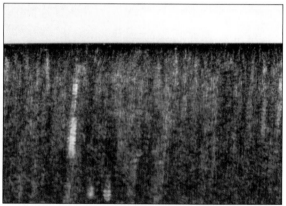

Smoothing a cutting edge

The quality of the cutting edge and finish on a tool blade depends on the size of abrasive particles used to sharpen it. Just as you would sand a tabletop with progressively finer grades of paper, sharpening begins with coarse abrasives and moves up through finer grits. The only difference is the size of abrasive particles involved. For example, a coarse India™ stone has particles measuring about 173 microns across, while a hard Arkansas oilstone has smaller particles—about 10 microns. Commerical honing compound used for buffing has extremely fine particles, as small as 0.5 micron. (By comparison, the diameter of a human hair is approximately 40 microns.) The photos above, of a chisel blade magnified approximately 200 times, reveal how sharpening improves a tool's edge. A dull chisel *(above, left)* has grooves and pits on its back and a nicked edge. These flaws will leave a rougher finish on wood than the smooth back and edge that is achieved after the chisel is sharpened and polished on a finish waterstone *(above, right)*.

The Sharpening Process Step-by-Step

Step 1: Grinding or Lapping

For badly scratched or nicked cutting edges, start the process by squaring the cutting edge, grinding the bevel, then lapping or flattening the back of the blade. Grinding is done with a bench grinder and coarse stones such as Washita; lap with rough abrasives or lapping compounds on a lapping plate.

Step 2: Sharpening

For tools that do not need grinding, sharpening can start here. Initial sharpening removes any roughness on the bevel and establishes a fine wire burr on the back of the blade. Sharpening is done by hand or with bevel-setting jigs on medium stones such as soft Arkansas.

Step 3: Honing

Honing uses progressively finer stones such as hard Arkansas or Japanese finishing stones to smooth out the scratches on the bevel caused by sharpening. Then the tool is turned over and lapped to remove the burr on the cutting edge. The microbevel *(below)* is also honed at this stage.

Step 4: Polishing

For a razor-sharp edge and a mirror-like finish, the tool can be polished with hard black Arkansas, ceramic or Japanese finish stones, as well as strops impregnated with fine buffing compounds.

Bevels and Microbevels

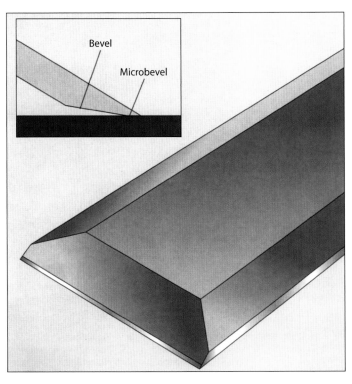

Bevel

Microbevel

Honing a microbevel

When a tool blade is razor-sharp, more force is necessary to drive the blade into the wood, and its edge is more likely to be brittle. By honing a secondary bevel, or microbevel, on top of the first *(inset)*, you can increase the cutting effectiveness of the tool and prolong the life of the cutting edge. Microbevels are slightly steeper than the original bevel of the tool. It can vary from as little as 2° to as much as 10°; the steeper the microbevel, the tougher the edge. Yet the microbevel should not be overworked. A few light strokes on a benchstone is usually sufficient to produce a small hairline strip at the edge of the main bevel *(left)*. If the microbevel is wider than half of the width of the bevel, the bevel should be reestablished by sharpening.

Sharpening Tools and Accessories

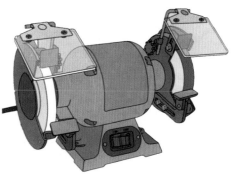

Bench grinder *(page 21)*
Medium-grit wheel *(left-hand side)* squares and grinds blade; cloth wheel *(right-hand side)* polishes cutting edge.

Honing compound
Applied to cloth wheel of grinder to polish sharpened bevel; contains a mixture of chromium dioxide and other fine abrasives.

Benchstone *(page 18)*
Any oilstone or waterstone used to hone or sharpen tools.

Neoprene polishing wheel
Rubber wheel for grinding and sharpening; available in grits between 90 and 240. Wheel must turn away from tool edge to prevent it from catching the edge.

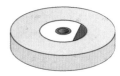

Aluminum oxide wheel
Standard wheel for grinding and sharpening; available in 6- and 8-inch sizes and a range of grits.

Dresser
Used to true or reshape grinder wheels and expose a fresh cutting surface. Star-wheel dresser *(above)* has up to four star-shaped wheels; diamond-point dresser *(below)* features a diamond set in a bronze tip.

Felt wheel
Available in soft, medium, and hard; dressed with buffing compound for final polishing of cutting edge.

Multi-tool jig
Skew-grinding jig *(right, top)* holds skews at 20° angle and pivots on center pin to grind radiused skew chisels. Sliding sharpening jig *(right, middle)* clamps tools under crossbar. Both are attached to an adjustable tool rest *(right, bottom)*, which mounts to bench in front of grinder.

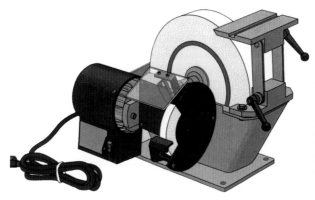

Wet/dry grinder *(page 21)*
Large, water-bathed wheel hones bevels; water prevents tools from overheating and carries away metal and grit. Smaller, dry wheel used for grinding.

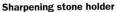

Auger bit file
Used to sharpen auger bits and other drill bits; one end has no teeth on edges and other end has teeth only on edges to prevent filing adjacent surfaces.

Single-cut bastard mill file
Used to sharpen spade bits and true the rims of Forstner bits.

Lapping compounds
Set of silicone carbide powders used in conjunction with a lapping plate to flatten and polish tool backs; grits range from 90 to 600.

Cant-saw file
Used in place of a three-square file in openings of less than 60°.

Three-square file
Triangular file used for sharpening Forstner and multi-spur bits.

Sharpening stone holder
Secures oilstones and waterstones up to 8 inches long for sharpening; rubber feet hold stone in place.

Angle checker
Brass guide for checking bevel and microbevel angles of sharpened tools; angles range from 15° to 120°.

Honing guide and angle jig
For honing plane blades. Device holds blade at appropriate angle for honing a bevel; rotating the wheel on top of the jig sets angles between 15° and 35°.

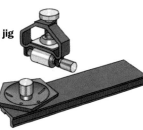

Diamond-coated honing files
Used to sharpen carbide router bits; stored inside their pivoting handles. Shown above from top: coarse, medium, and fine files.

Bit files
Boron-carbide stones used to sharpen router bits; gives a finer finish than diamond honing files of equal grit. Handle features magnifying lens for checking sharpness.

Strop
A leather strip glued to a handle; dressed with commercial honing compound or other fine abrasives to polish a sharpened edge.

Diamond needle file
Small half-round file used for sharpening band-saw blades.

Waterstone storage unit
Plastic reservoir used to immerse up to four waterstones for storage between sharpenings; features clamps that can be flipped up to hold the waterstone for sharpening or honing and a glass lapping plate.

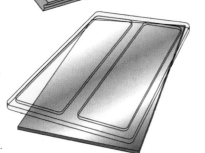

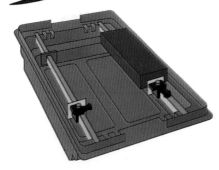

Benchstones

The benchstone is the most commonly found sharpening accessory in the shop. Once referred to as natural stones, benchstones now encompass many man-made materials, ranging from aluminum oxide to ceramics. Many "stones" include fine diamond bonded to steel.

Sharpening stones are generally divided into two groups according to the lubricant used with them: oil and water. Lubrication serves to disperse ground particles and prevent them from clogging the stone. Choosing between the two is mostly a matter of feel; some woodworkers prefer the edge a glassy hard black Arkansas oilstone gives a tool; others like the fine control a softer Japanese finish waterstone offers.

Naturally occurring oilstones have long been regarded as the finest sharpening stones. Quarried from novaculite and sold as Washita and Arkansas stones, these sharpening surfaces are becoming scarce. If your budget permits, natural stones are a good investment; they will last a lifetime.

Synthetic substitutes made of aluminum oxide (India™ stones) or silicon carbide (Crystolon™) are less expensive and just as effective as natural stones, though they tend to wear more quickly. An economical compromise is the use of an India™ stone for rough sharpening and whetting, and a hard Arkansas stone for honing and polishing. When using oilstones, wipe them often with a rag to prevent glazing. Do not use a heavy oil, as it inhibits the abrading process; a light machine oil cut with kerosene works best.

Waterstones are Japanese in origin, and cut much faster than oilstones. Because they use water, rather than oil as the lubricant, there is no oily mess left on clothes and workpieces. Waterstones come in finer grades than oilstones, making them popular with woodworkers who like to hone and polish. Because they are softer than oilstones, new abrasive is constantly exposed during use, and the slurry formed by the water will form a fine polishing paste.

Waterstones have their drawbacks, however. Because they are softer than oilstones, they must be trued more often *(page 19)*.

Tools should be dried and wiped with oil thoroughly after sharpening to prevent rust. Waterstones also should be stored in water. If your shop is prone to cold temperatures, keep your waterstones from freezing, as they will shatter.

A Collection of Benchstones

Oilstones

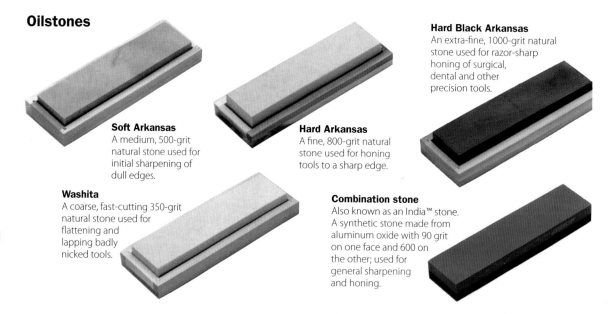

Soft Arkansas
A medium, 500-grit natural stone used for initial sharpening of dull edges.

Washita
A coarse, fast-cutting 350-grit natural stone used for flattening and lapping badly nicked tools.

Hard Arkansas
A fine, 800-grit natural stone used for honing tools to a sharp edge.

Hard Black Arkansas
An extra-fine, 1000-grit natural stone used for razor-sharp honing of surgical, dental and other precision tools.

Combination stone
Also known as an India™ stone. A synthetic stone made from aluminum oxide with 90 grit on one face and 600 on the other; used for general sharpening and honing.

18

Truing a Benchstone

Lapping compound

Slurry

Lapping table

Flattening the stone

All benchstones will develop a hollow in the center after prolonged use. To true a benchstone, flatten it on a machined surface, such as glass pane or a lapping table. For oilstones, rub the surface with a circular motion *(left)* in a slurry made from a coarse lapping compound mixed with honing oil. Start with a coarse grit and work through finer grits until the stone is flat. To true a waterstone, use water instead of honing oil for the slurry, or wet/dry silicon carbide paper taped to the lapping surface.

Waterstones

Japanese finishing stone
An extra-fine, 1200-grit synthetic stone made from cerium oxide; used for final honing and polishing; small Nagura stone used to create slurry.

Japanese coarse stone
A coarse, l80-grlt synthetic stone made from silicone carbide; used for flattening and lapping badly nicked tools.

Other Stones

Slipstone
A shaped stone used for turning and carving tools, featuring both rounded and angled edges; a range of grits is available in both oil and water types.

Gouge slipstone
A conical stone used for gouges; concave surface sharpens outside edge of tool, while convex surface deburrs the inside edge. A range of grits is available in both oil and water types.

Diamond stone
A hard synthetic stone made from microscopic diamond crystals bonded to solid steel plate; features a true, flat surface that will not wear like other stones. Available in a range of grits between 220 and 1200 for any sharpening or honing task.

Ceramic stone
A fine, hard 1000-grit synthetic stone made from bonded aluminum oxide; used for honing. Needs no lubricant.

Bench Grinders

From squaring and sharpening plane irons to polishing chisels and turning tools, the bench grinder is a worthwhile addition to a woodworking shop's sharpening station.

Bench grinders are classified according to their wheel diameter. Standard 5-to 8-inch benchtop models, with ¼- to ¾-horsepower motors, are the most popular sizes. Larger wheels are better, as smaller wheels can produce exaggerated hollow-ground bevels. Grinders can be mounted on a work surface or fastened to a separate stand.

Rotating around 3500 rpm, a bench grinder removes steel faster than a sharpening stone. Unfortunately, it also heats up the tool, and you may lose the tool's temper. If the steel begins to change color during grinding, deepening to a true blue, the temper has been lost, and the tool must be reground. Motorized whetstones and wet/dry grinders feature water-bathed wheels that turn at slower speeds, such as 500 rpm, allowing you to grind tools without constantly dipping them in water for cooling.

Most grinders can be equipped with optional rubber sharpening wheels, cloth buffing wheels, and leather strop wheels in addition to standard abrasive wheels, which come in a variety of grits *(page 22)*. Grinding wheels will eventually become dull and clogged with metal particles, and their edges may go out of square. A wheel dresser *(page 22)* can be used to true the face of a glazed wheel and square its edges.

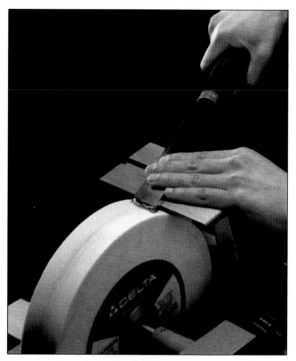

The cutting edge of a skew chisel gets a sharpening on a wet/dry grinder. Because the large wheel of this type of grinder rotates relatively slowly and is continually bathed in water, the blade being sharpened remains cool, which reduces the risk of destroying its temper. Standard bench grinder wheels often rotate at speeds that are too fast for honing many tools; as a result, the tool's steel can easily overheat.

Shop Tip

Reversing wheel guards for buffing

Because they spin in the same direction as the standard grinding wheel mounted on the left-hand side of a bench grinder, neoprene or felt buffing wheels mounted on the right-hand require a change of tool position for buffing so the tool does not catch in the wheel. Another solution is to reverse the right-hand wheel guard to expose the rear of the wheel *(right)*. In this position, the buffing wheel spins away from you instead of towards you, so you can buff the tool at the same angle as you do when grinding it.

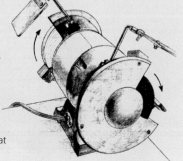

Standard Bench Grinder

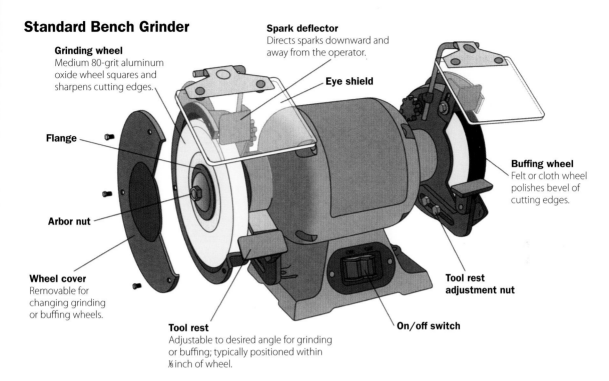

Grinding wheel
Medium 80-grit aluminum oxide wheel squares and sharpens cutting edges.

Spark deflector
Directs sparks downward and away from the operator.

Eye shield

Flange

Arbor nut

Buffing wheel
Felt or cloth wheel polishes bevel of cutting edges.

Wheel cover
Removable for changing grinding or buffing wheels.

Tool rest
Adjustable to desired angle for grinding or buffing; typically positioned within ⅛ inch of wheel.

Tool rest adjustment nut

On/off switch

Wet/Dry Grinder

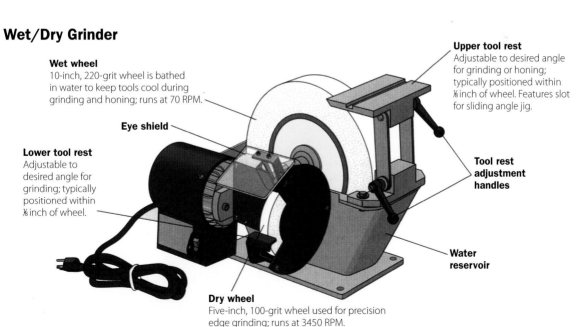

Wet wheel
10-inch, 220-grit wheel is bathed in water to keep tools cool during grinding and honing; runs at 70 RPM.

Upper tool rest
Adjustable to desired angle for grinding or honing; typically positioned within ⅛ inch of wheel. Features slot for sliding angle jig.

Eye shield

Lower tool rest
Adjustable to desired angle for grinding; typically positioned within ⅛ inch of wheel.

Tool rest adjustment handles

Water reservoir

Dry wheel
Five-inch, 100-grit wheel used for precision edge grinding; runs at 3450 RPM.

Identifying Grinder Wheels

Standard Marking System Chart			
Abrasive Type	**A**: Aluminum oxide	**C**: Silicon carbide	**Z**: Aluminum zirconium
Abrasive (Grain) Size	**Coarse**: 8, 10, 12, 14,16, 20, 24	**Medium**: 30, 36, 46, 54, 60	**Fine**: 70, 80, 90, 100, 120, 150, 180 **Very fine**: 220, 240, 280, 320, 400, 500, 600
Grade Scale	Soft A B C D E F G H I J K L M N O P Q R S T U V W X Y Z	Medium	Hard
Structure	Dense ⟶ Open 1 2 3 4 5 6 7 8 9 10 11 12 13 14 15 16 etc		
Bond	**B**: Resinoid **BF**: Resinoid reinforced **E**: Shellac **O**: Oxychloride **R**: Rubber		
Type	**RF**: Rubber reinforced **S**: Silicate **V**: Vitrified		

Courtesy of the American National Standards Institute

Choosing a grinder wheel

The wheels supplied on grinders are usually too coarse for use with finer tools. A wide variety of replacement stones are available, but selecting the right one is no simple matter. You need to decipher the codes marked on the sides of the wheels, describing their composition and abrasive quality. The chart above will help you interpret these codes. (They are usually found sandwiched between two numerical manufacturer's symbols printed on the side of the stone.) If you plan to use a wheel to grind carbon-steel tools, and then hone with a benchstone, buy a wheel marked A 80 H 8V. This means the wheel is aluminum oxide (A), fine-grained (80), and relatively soft (H), with a medium structure or concentration of abrasives (8). The particles are bonded together by a process of heat and fusion known as vitrification (V). For high-speed steel tools, a medium hardness of I or J is better. If you plan to use your tools right off the grinder, choose a wheel with a grain size of 100 or 120.

Dressing a Grinding Wheel

Truing the wheel

A grinding wheel should be trued when ridges or hollows appear on the stone or if it becomes discolored. You can use either a star-wheel or diamond-point dresser. To use a star-wheel dresser *(right)*, move the grinder's tool rest away from the wheel. With the guard in position, switch on the grinder and butt the tip of the dresser against the wheel. Then, with your index finger resting against the tool rest, move the dresser from side to side. To use a diamond-point dresser, hold the device between the index finger and the thumb of one hand, set it on the tool rest, and advance it toward the wheel until your index finger contacts the tool rest. Move either dresser back and forth across the wheel until the edges are square and you have exposed fresh abrasive.

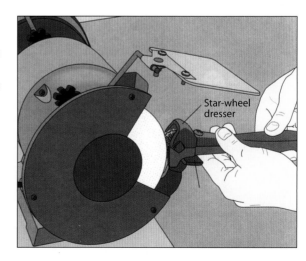

Star-wheel dresser

A Mobile Sharpening Dolly

A sharpening station is more than just a dedicated space for sharpening. It is a way of keeping all of your benchstones, grinding jigs, and sharpening accessories clean and well-organized. The sharpening station shown below is essentially a sturdy low bench with a storage shelf. The unit is built from ¾-inch plywood and 1-by-3 stock. By adding locking casters, it becomes a mobile sharpening dolly that you can wheel about the shop to wherever you need to sharpen: at the lathe, the carving bench, or near the sink.

To build the dolly, cut the base from ¾-inch plywood. Make it large enough to incorporate all your sharpening gear so that it is not too cluttered; up to 3-by-6 feet is a good size. Screw four corner blocks to the underside of the base, and fasten a locking caster on each block.

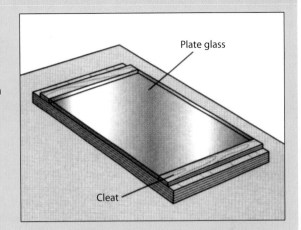

Plate glass

Cleat

To strengthen the dolly, cut the pieces for the skirts and legs from 1-by-3 stock. The legs should be long enough for the top to sit at a comfortable height; between 32 and 36 inches is right for most people.

Screw the leg pieces together, then attach the skirts to the legs' inside faces. Fasten the shelf and the top to the skirts. If desired, glue a water-and-oil-proof plastic laminate work surface to the top.

Once you have built the dolly, mount a standard bench grinder or wet/dry grinder to the end of the bench so that both wheels are accessible. Secure a lapping table *(inset)* at the opposite end for lapping and flattening stones. This is simply a piece of ⅜-inch tempered plate glass secured with cleats to a piece of ½-inch plywood, fastened to the top. Have the glass cut three times larger than your largest bench stone.

Now mount your most commonly used benchstones either by using cleats or screwing their wooden storage boxes to the tabletop; countersink the fasteners. Other accessories could include a vise or a portable light positioned to shine on the grinder.

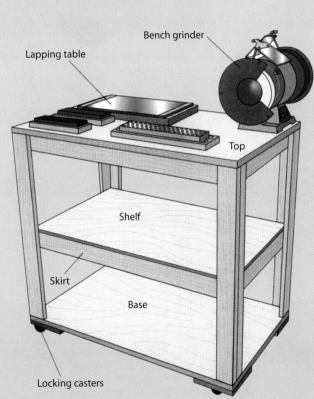

Lapping table

Bench grinder

Top

Shelf

Skirt

Base

Locking casters

Maintaining Hand Tools

Despite the proliferation of power tools in recent years, hand tools are still an important part of the modern woodworking shop. Handsaws, chisels, and planes play a vital role in many cabinetmaking tasks, from cutting joints and chopping mortises to smoothing stock. For some crafts, like carving and turning, hand-cutting tools such as gouges and skew chisels are virtually indispensable.

One distinct advantage that hand tools offer over their electrically powered counterparts is that they are relatively straightforward to sharpen and maintain. With hand tools, there are no hidden circuit boards or sealed components, no carbide-tipped blades that must be sharpened professionally. With most hand tools, such as saws and chisels, what you see is what you get: a handle, often made of wood, and a steel cutting edge. True, not all hand tools are quite this simple. Bench planes feature screws and levers for adjusting the angle and position of the cutting edge. Still, all the parts are easily accessible, allowing you to sharpen and maintain the tool in the shop. In fact, with a little elbow grease and the right materials, you can even restore a rusty old hand plane to better condition than when it was first bought *(page 40)*.

Setting yourself up for hand tool sharpening and maintenance requires no great investment. All you need are solvents for cleaning, a few commercial devices for adjusting blades, stones and files for honing and sharpening—and the proper technique. The following pages will show you how to care for and sharpen the most commonly used hand tools, from handsaws *(page 26)* and chisels and gouges *(page 30)* to bench planes *(page 39)*, scrapers *(page 46)*, and bits for braces and hand drills *(page 55)*.

The work is relatively easy, but the rewards are considerable. Hand tools that are well sharpened and properly maintained will improve the quality of your projects and prolong the life of your tools.

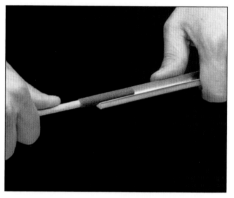

The simple shop-made jig shown above, consisting of a dowel wrapped in a piece of emery cloth, is ideal for cleaning and removing burrs from the rounded edge of gouges.

The cutting edge of a drawknife is honed by an axe-stone. Holding one handle of the tool as shown at left and butting the other handle against the crook of the arm exposes the entire edge for sharpening.

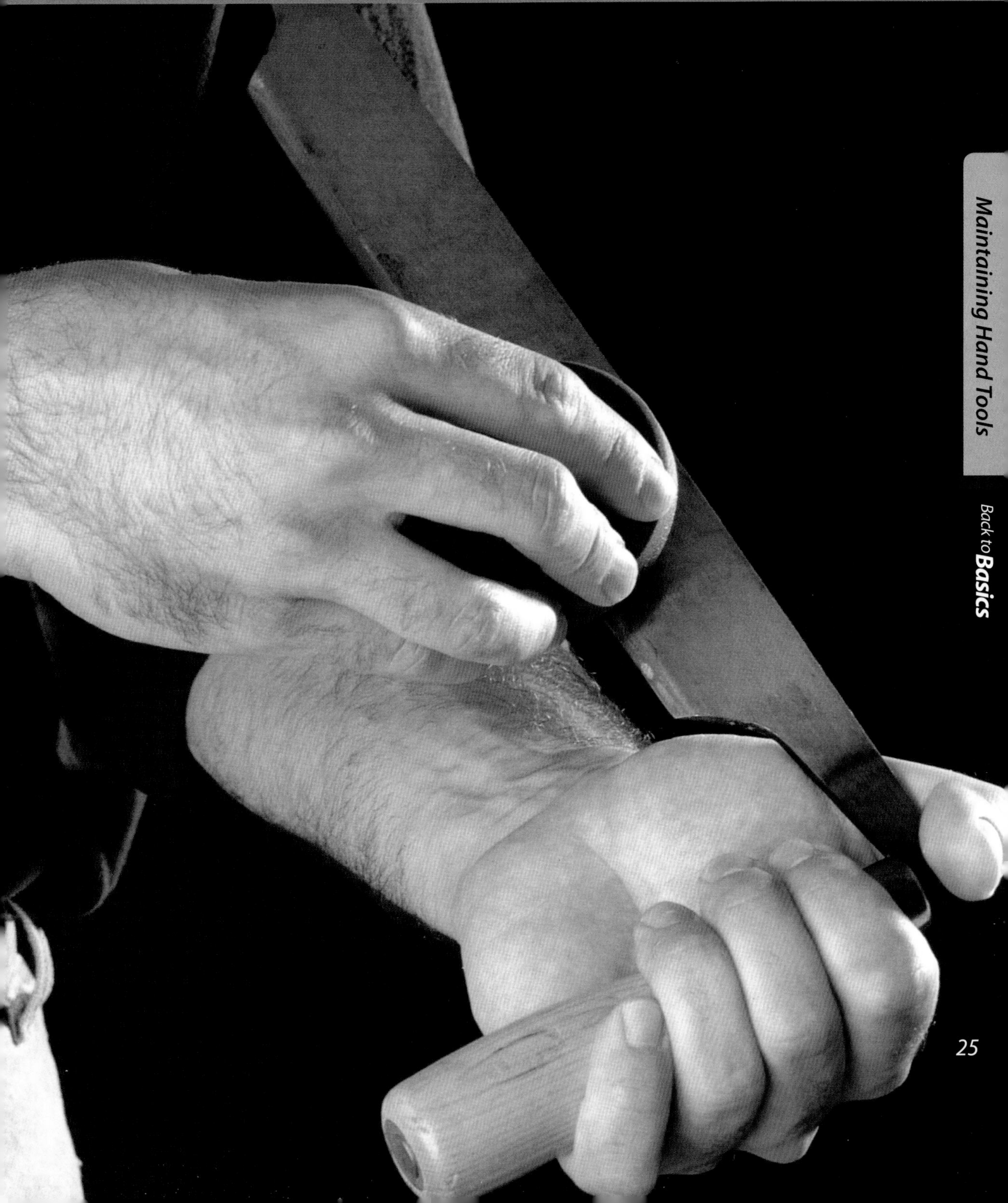

Handsaws

Sharpening a handsaw is a three-step operation. As shown on page 28, the process begins with jointing, or filing the tips of the teeth so that they are all the same height. This is followed by setting the teeth to the correct angle. This ensures that the blade cuts straight and does not stick in the kerf. Setting involves bending the teeth alternately to each side of the blade's centerline. The final step in the process is sharpening itself, typically with a file.

Not all handsaws are identical. The shape, spacing, and set of the teeth vary according to the type of cutting the saw will perform. The spacing between teeth is usually expressed in TPI, or teeth per inch. The following pages describe how to sharpen rip saws, combination saws, and both Japanese and Western-style crosscut saws. Because of their very fine teeth, dovetail and tenon saws should be sent out to a professional for sharpening.

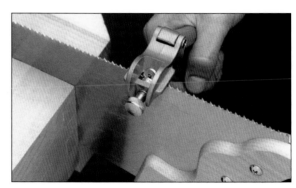

A commercial saw set bends the teeth of a combination saw to the proper angle with the blade clamped in a bench vise. Setting the teeth of a saw blade is a key step in the sharpening process, producing a kerf that prevents the blade from binding.

Anatomy of Saw Blades and Filing Angles

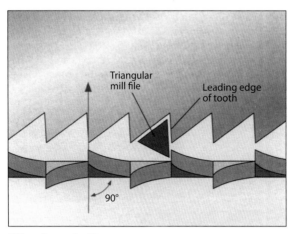

Filing ripsaw teeth
Ripsaws have widely spaced teeth with from five to seven teeth per inch (TPI). They also have a more pronounced set than other saws. Both features enable them to cut quickly along the grain. As shown above, the leading edges of rip teeth are almost vertical. To sharpen the teeth, use a triangular mill file, drawing it straight across each tooth at a 90° angle to the blade axis.

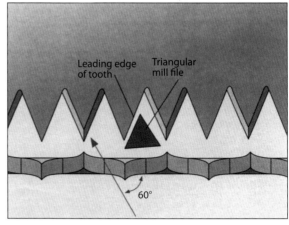

Filing combination teeth
Combination saws are dual-purpose saws that can be used for both rip cuts and crosscuts, although they rip more slowly than a rip saw and cut more roughly than a crosscut saw. Combination teeth slope forward and backward at the same angle (about 60°) and both edges are beveled. Sharpen both edges using a triangular mill file *(above)*, tilting the handle of the file down slightly.

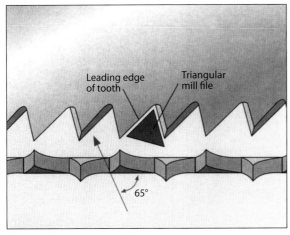

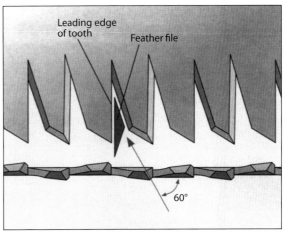

Sharpening crosscut teeth

The teeth of a crosscut saw are closely spaced—eight to 12 TPI is typical—and they have very little set. Crosscut teeth feature sloped leading edges with bevels, which enable them to cut cleanly across the grain. As with rip saws, the teeth are sharpened with a triangular mill file. Hold the file at the same angle as the bevel, which is typically 65° *(above)*.

Sharpening Japanese crosscut teeth

Japanese saws, which cut on the pull stroke, have tall, narrow teeth with very little set. Also, the teeth are beveled on leading and trailing edges, and on the tips. All edges should be sharpened with a feather file held at about a 60° angle to the blade *(above)*.

Shop Tip

A saw holder
Storing handsaws properly will both eliminate clutter and keep the tools accessible and safe from damage. The simple device shown here can be used to hang a saw on the shop wall in plain view. Cut a wood scrap a little thicker than the saw handle to the same profile as the opening in the handle; use the opening as a template, Fasten the piece to the wall at a convenient height, then screw a small block with rounded ends to the piece as a turn-buckle. Make the turnbuckle shorter than the width of the handle opening, but longer than the height. Leave the screw slightly loose so that you can pivot the turnbuckle vertically to secure the saw to the wall.

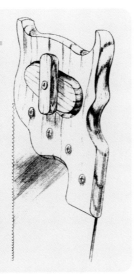

A Bench Vise Saw Holder

Secured in a vise, the simple jig shown at left will hold a saw at a convenient height for sharpening. Make the jaws from two pieces of ½-inch plywood about 10 inches long and 7 inches wide. Then saw two ⅛-inch-thick strips and glue them along the inside faces of the jaws, flush with the top end; the strips will grip the saw blade. Fasten the two jaws together near the bottom end, screwing a strip of ⅛-inch plywood between them. Finally, bore a hole for a carriage bolt through the middle of the jaws and install the bolt with a washer and wing nut.

To use the jig, secure the bottom end in your vise. Loosen the wing nut, slip a saw blade between the jaws, and tighten the nut to hold the saw securely.

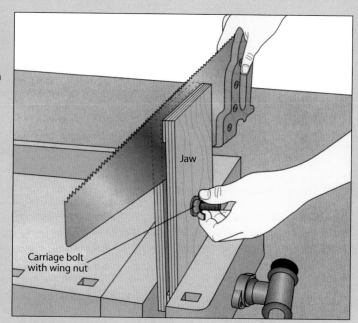

Jaw

Carriage bolt with wing nut

Sharpening a Handsaw

Jointing the teeth

Mount the saw teeth-up in a vise with a wood pad on each side of the blade for protection. Install a flat mill bastard file in a commercial saw jointing jig. Hold the jig flat against the side of the blade and pass the file back and forth across the full length of the teeth *(right)*. This will flatten all of the teeth to the same height. A few passes should be sufficient.

Saw jointer

Wood pad

Setting the teeth

With the saw still in the vise, adjust a saw set to the same TPI as the blade. Starting at either end of the blade, position the first tooth that is bent away from you between the anvil and the punch block. Squeeze the handle to set the tooth *(right)*. Work your way down the length of the blade, setting all teeth that are bent away from you. Then turn the saw around in the vise and repeat the process on the remaining teeth.

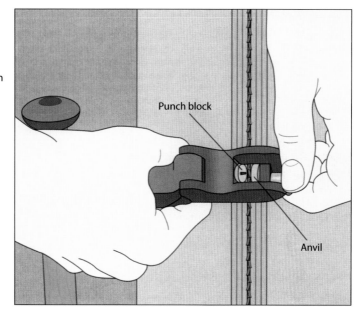

Punch block

Anvil

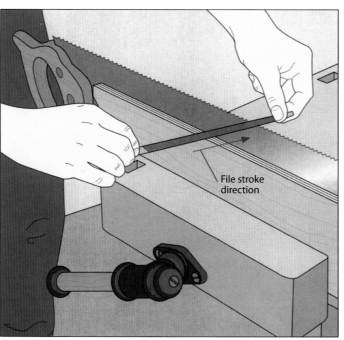

File stroke direction

Filing the teeth

Refer to the appropriate illustration on page 26 or 27 for the proper file and filing angle for the saw you are sharpening. For the crosscut saw shown at left, hold a triangular file at about a 65° angle to the blade with its handle tilted down slightly. As you file the teeth, work from one end of the blade to the other, filing all the teeth that are set in one direction. Then turn the saw around to sharpen the remaining teeth.

Chisels and Gouges

Chisels and gouges must have razor-sharp edges to work properly. Sharpening a standard woodworking chisel is simple; all you need is a combination sharpening stone. For most chisels and gouges, you will have to hone and polish the cutting edge as well as produce the correct bevel angle for the blade.

Well-sharpened blades are essential for turning chisels and gouges. Dull cutting edges not only produce poor results; they are also more difficult to control and dangerous to use. This section of the chapter explains how to sharpen and refurbish a wide range of chisels and gouges.

Even the most rusted and pitted blade can be renewed with steel wool, mineral spirits, clean rags, and a bit of elbow grease.

Inventory of Chisels and Gouges

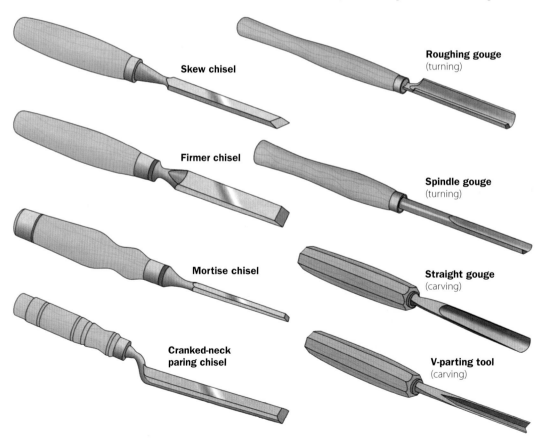

Skew chisel

Firmer chisel

Mortise chisel

Cranked-neck paring chisel

Roughing gouge
(turning)

Spindle gouge
(turning)

Straight gouge
(carving)

V-parting tool
(carving)

Replacing a Chisel or Gouge Handle

Turning the new handle

Turn a new handle for a chisel or gouge on the lathe. Cut a blank from a dense, strong hardwood like ash or hickory. The grain should run the length of the blank. A piece that is 1½ to 2 inches square and a few inches longer than the finished length you need will yield a suitable handle. Mount the piece between centers on the lathe and turn it to a smooth cylinder using a roughing gouge. Buy a brass ferrule for the handle. Then use a parting tool to turn a tenon on one end of the blank to accommodate the ferrule. Measure the inside diameter of the ferrule with dial calipers *(right)* and size the tenon to fit tightly.

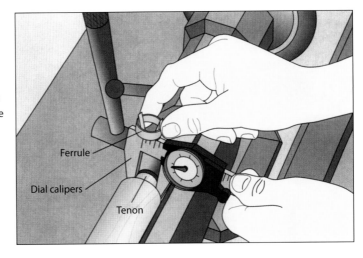

Ferrule

Dial calipers

Tenon

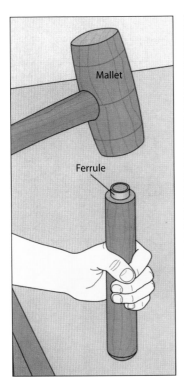

Mallet

Ferrule

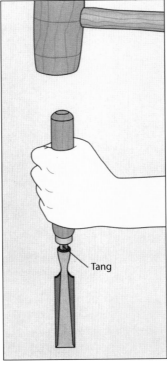

Tang

Mounting the ferrule and the blade

Remove the handle from the lathe, set it end-down on a work surface, and tap the ferrule in place with a mallet *(far left)*. Next, remount the handle on the lathe and shape it with a skew chisel and spindle gouge. Once you are satisfied with the handle's shape and feel, bore a hole in the tenon end to accommodate the tang of the blade. Bore the hole on the lathe with a Jacobs chuck attached to the tailstock; make sure the hole is centered in the blank. The hole's diameter and depth depend on the type of tang. For a round-section, untapered tang, the hole should be 2 to 3 inches deep and equal to the tang diameter. For a square-section, tapered tang, drill two holes as you would counterbore for a screw and plug: Make the top half the same diameter as the tang 1¼ inches from the tip and the bottom half the same width as the tang ¾ inch from its tip. Insert the blade into the handle and rap the butt end of the handle with a mallet *(near left)*.

Sharpening a Standard Chisel

Cleats

Microbevel

Honing the cutting edge

The two-step procedure shown on this page can be used to sharpen any standard chisel, such as a firmer, paring, or mortise chisel. Start by honing a secondary bevel on the forward edge of the existing one—called a microbevel (inset)—then polish and flatten the back side of the blade. To form the microbevel, lay a combination stone coarse-side up on a work surface between two cleats secured with screws. Saturate the stone with the appropriate lubricant, if necessary, until it pools on the surface. Holding the blade with the existing bevel flat on the stone, raise it about 5° and slide the cutting edge along the stone in long, elliptical passes (left). Apply moderate pressure until a microbevel forms. Turn the stone over and make a few passes on the fine side.

Polishing and flattening the back side of the blade

Saturate the fine side of the stone and, holding the chisel blade flat on the stone, bevel-side up, move it in a circular pattern (right) until the flat side of the cutting edge is smooth.

Sharpening a Roughing-Out Gouge

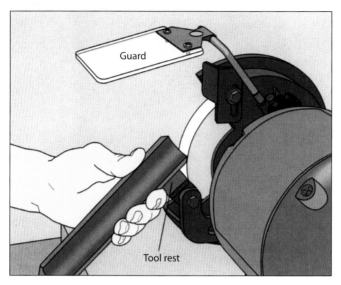

Guard

Tool rest

Grinding the cutting edge

Sharpen a roughing-out gouge on a bench grinder equipped with a medium grinding wheel and a felt wheel. Position the guard and turn on the machine. Holding the blade between the fingers and thumb of one hand, set the cutting edge on the tool rest and advance it until the bevel lightly contacts the grinding wheel. To change the bevel angle of the cutting edge, adjust the tool rest to the desired angle. With your index finger against the tool rest, roll the blade on the wheel *(left)* until the entire edge is ground. Keep the bevel flat against the wheel at all times. Continue, checking the blade regularly, until the cutting edge is sharp and the bevel angle is correct. To prevent the blade from overheating, occasionally dip it in water if it is carbon steel, or remove it from the wheel if it is high-speed steel to let it cool down.

Maintaining Hand Tools

Back to **Basics**

Gouge-Sharpening Jig

The jig shown at right will hold most turning gouges so the blade contacts the grinding wheel at the correct angle. Cut the base and guide from ½-inch plywood. Screw the guide together and fasten it to the base with countersunk screws from underneath. Make the guide opening large enough for the arm to slide through freely.

Cut the arm from 1-by-2 stock and the tool support from ½-inch plywood. Screw the two parts of the tool support together, then fasten the bottom to the arm flush with one end. For the V-block, cut a small block to size and saw a 90° wedge out of one side. Glue the piece to the tool support.

To use the jig, secure it to a work surface so the arm lines up directly under the grinding wheel. Seat the gouge handle in the V-block and slide the arm so the beveled edge of the gouge sits flat on the grinding wheel. Clamp the arm in place. Then, with the gouge clear of the wheel, switch on the grinder and reposition the tool on the jig. Roll the beveled edge across the wheel *(right, bottom)*.

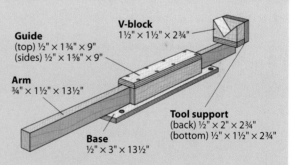

Guide
(top) ½" × 1¾" × 9"
(sides) ½" × 1⅝" × 9"

Arm
¾" × 1½" × 13½"

V-block
1½" × 1½" × 2¾"

Tool support
(back) ½" × 2" × 2¾"
(bottom) ½" × 1½" × 2¾"

Base
½" × 3" × 13½"

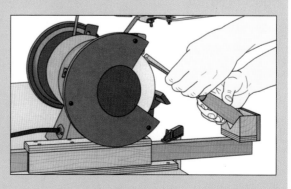

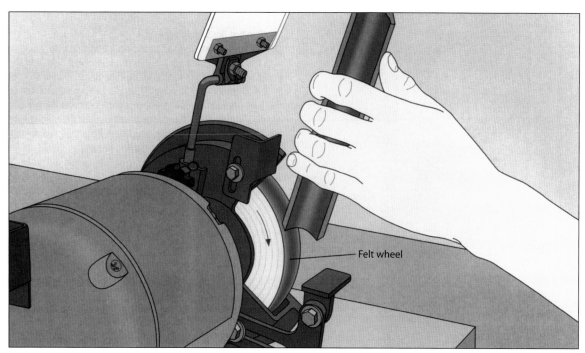

Felt wheel

Shop Tip

Shop-made honing guides and rust removers

The inside edges of gouges can be difficult to hone and strop if you do not have a slipstone or strop with the correct shape. You can make a gouge-honing guide by wrapping a dowel with 600-grit sandpaper (near right). For stropping, simply fold a strip of leather to fit the inside edge of the gouge (far right). You can also use these jigs to clean rust or pitting from an old blade.

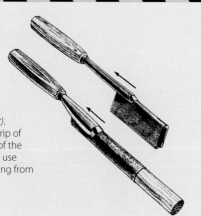

Polishing the cutting edge

Shift to the grinder's felt wheel and move the tool rest out of the way. Hold a stick of polishing compound against the felt wheel to impregnate it with abrasive. Grip the handle of the gouge in your right hand and hold the blade between the fingers and thumbs of your left hand. Then, with the gouge almost vertical, set the bevel flat against the wheel. Lightly roll the blade from side to side against the wheel to polish the bevel. A slight burr will form on the inside edge of the tool. To feel for the burr, run your finger gently across the inside edge of the blade. To remove it, roll the inside face of the blade against the wheel until the burr rubs off. Avoid overbuffing the blade; this will dull the cutting edge. Test the tool for sharpness by cutting a scrap across the grain. The blade should produce a clean shaving.

34

A Spindle Gouge

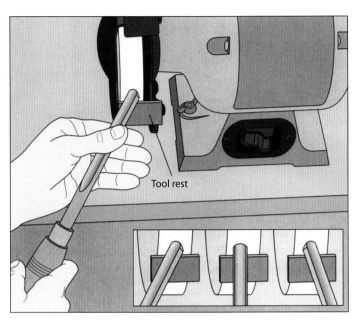

Tool rest

Sharpening on a bench grinder

Position the guard properly and turn on the grinder. Holding the blade between the fingers and thumb of one hand, set the blade flat on the tool rest and advance it until the blade lightly touches the stone *(left)*. Adjust the tool rest to create the desired bevel angle. Roll the cutting edge on the wheel and pivot the handle from left to right while keeping the bevel flat on the grinding wheel at all times *(inset)*. Continue rolling the blade and moving the tool handle from side to side until the edge is sharpened, stopping frequently to check the grind and cool the tip. Hone the cutting edge and remove the burr by hand, as shown below, or use the grinder's felt wheel *(page 34)*.

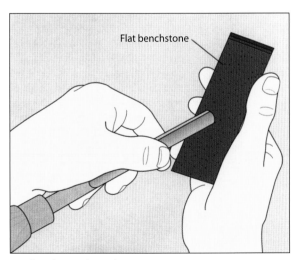

Flat benchstone

Covex slipstone

OIL

Honing the cutting edge

Once the bevel has been sharpened on the grinder, use a flat benchstone to polish the tool to a razor-sharp edge. Saturate the stone with oil, then roll the outside bevel across the abrasive surface *(above)* to hone the bevel on the cutting edge.

Removing the burr

Use a convex slipstone matching the curvature of the gouge to remove the burr that forms on the inside of the cutting edge. Lubricate the slipstone if needed and hone the inside edge until the burr is eliminated.

Maintaining Hand Tools

Back to **Basics**

35

Sharpening a Carving Gouge

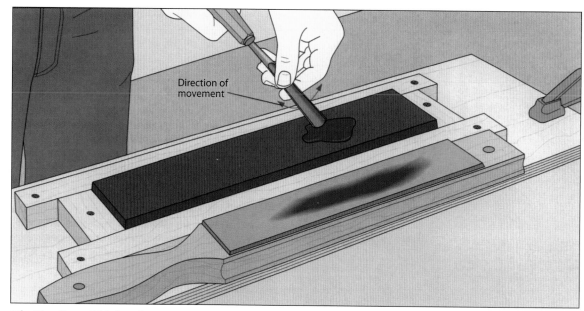

Direction of movement

Whetting the outside bevel

Set an oilstone on a plywood base, screw cleats to the base around the stone to keep it from moving, and clamp the base to a work surface. (The leather strop is used to polish the outside bevel). Saturate the stone, then set the outside bevel of the gouge flat on it. Starting at one end, move the blade back and forth along the stone with a rhythmic motion, simultaneously rolling the tool so the entire bevel contacts the sharpening surface *(above)*. Avoid rocking the blade too far, as this will tend to round over its corners and blunt the cutting edge. Continue until the bevel is smooth and a burr forms on the inside edge of the blade. You can also carry out this step on a grinder, as shown on page 33, but if you use the machine be sure to adjust the angle of the tool rest to match the bevel angle of the gouge.

Honing an inside bevel

Once you have sharpened the gouge's outside bevel, use a conical slipstone to hone a slight inside bevel on the blade and to remove the burr that has formed. Put a few drops of oil on the cutting edge of the gouge. Then, holding the stone on a work surface, move the blade back and forth along the stone making sure that you keep the cutting edge well away from your fingers. Continue until the burr is removed and an inside bevel of approximately 5° forms.

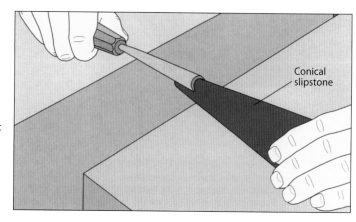

Conical slipstone

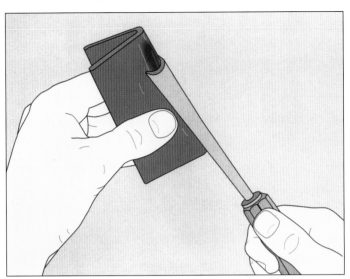

Polishing the inside bevel

Use a folded piece of leather to strop the inside bevel of the gouge. Spread some polishing compound on the leather and fold it so its edge matches the inside curve of the gouge. Draw the blade along the leather repeatedly to polish the inside bevel *(left)*. This can also be done using the felt wheel of a bench grinder.

Polishing the outside bevel

Spread some polishing compound on the strop and use the same rolling technique shown before to polish the outside bevel *(above)*. Check the inside bevel; if a burr has formed, repolish inside. You can also use a bench grinder and a felt wheel impregnated with polishing compound *(page 34)* for this task.

Sharpening a V-Tool

Whetting the outside edges

Sharpen each side of a V-tool separately. Set up and saturate an oilstone as you would to sharpen a carving gouge *(page 36)*. Hone one outside bevel of the V-tool as you would a chisel *(page 32)*, moving the blade back and forth along the length of the stone and keeping the bevel flat on the stone. Repeat on the other side of the V *(right)*. Stop working when you have removed the rough marks from the ground edge and a small burr forms on the inside of the edge.

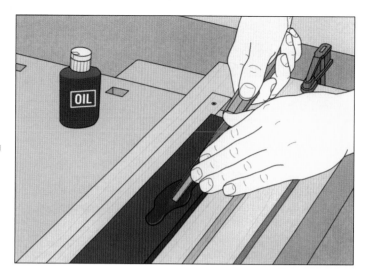

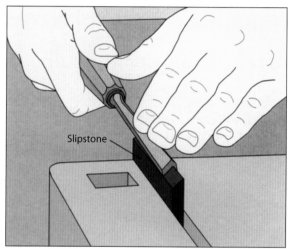

Removing the hook

When you sharpen the outside bevels of a V-tool, a hook of excess metal will form at the apex of the V *(inset)*. This hook must be ground away before you hone the inside bevel. Holding the tool on the stone, roll the corner across the surface *(above)*. Move the tool from end to end along the stone until you wear away the hook and an outside bevel forms at the apex of the V, forming one continuous beveled edge. This process will create a burr in the center of the inside edge, which will be removed.

Honing the inside bevel

To remove the burr and hone an inside bevel, use a triangular slipstone that matches the angle of the V-tool blade as closely as possible. Clamp the stone securely in a bench vise and saturate it with oil. To avoid crushing the stone, do not overtighten the vise. Draw the end of the blade's inside edge back and forth along the stone *(above)*, applying light downward pressure until the burr is removed and a slight inside bevel forms. To finish, polish the edge with a leather strop *(page 37)* or the felt wheel of a grinder *(page 34)*.

Slipstone

Bench Planes

A good-quality bench plane can be costly, but there is no reason why it should not last a lifetime—or two. This section shows how to care for a plane, and includes information on sharpening and adjusting the tool. You can save yourself some money—without sacrificing a whit of quality—by refurbishing an old plane *(page 40)*. Even a tool that has been abused and discarded by someone else can be brought back to life.

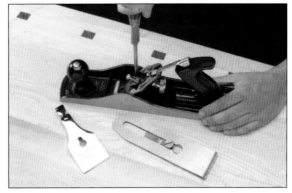

Tightening the frog setscrews is a fundamental step in the reassembly of the bench plane *(page 45)*.

Anatomy of a Bench Plane

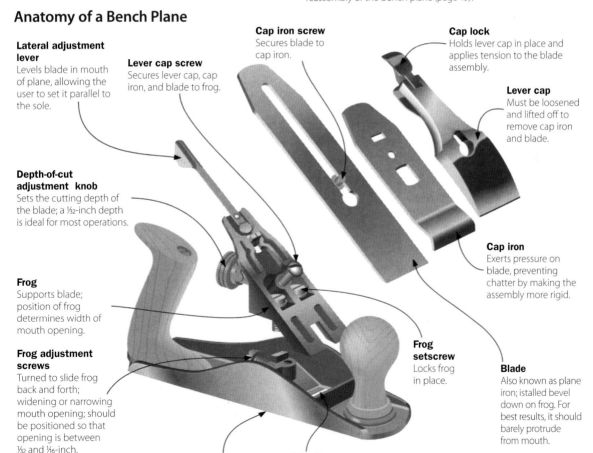

Lateral adjustment lever
Levels blade in mouth of plane, allowing the user to set it parallel to the sole.

Lever cap screw
Secures lever cap, cap iron, and blade to frog.

Cap iron screw
Secures blade to cap iron.

Cap lock
Holds lever cap in place and applies tension to the blade assembly.

Lever cap
Must be loosened and lifted off to remove cap iron and blade.

Depth-of-cut adjustment knob
Sets the cutting depth of the blade; a ½-inch depth is ideal for most operations.

Cap iron
Exerts pressure on blade, preventing chatter by making the assembly more rigid.

Frog
Supports blade; position of frog determines width of mouth opening.

Frog adjustment screws
Turned to slide frog back and forth; widening or narrowing mouth opening; should be positioned so that opening is between ½₂ and ¼₆-inch.

Frog setscrew
Locks frog in place.

Blade
Also known as plane iron; istalled bevel down on frog. For best results, it should barely protrude from mouth.

Sole

Mouth

39

Refurbishing a Bench Plane

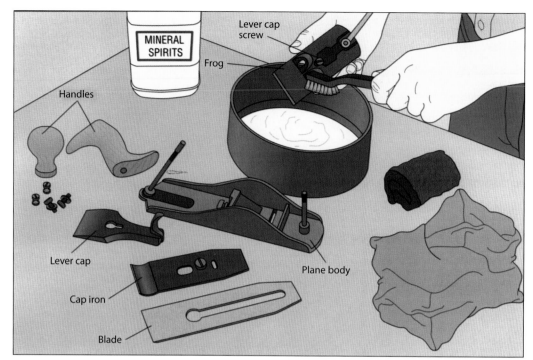

MINERAL SPIRITS

Lever cap screw

Frog

Handles

Lever cap

Cap iron

Blade

Plane body

Dissassembling and cleaning the plane

Refer to the anatomy illustration on page 39 to help you take the plane apart. Start by loosening the lever cap screw and releasing the cap lock, then take off the lever cap, cap iron, and blade and set them aside. Next, loosen and remove the frog setscrews and separate the frog from the sole of the plane. You can also unscrew the front and back handles from the body. Clean each part individually using a brass-bristled brush dipped in mineral spirits *(above)*.

Lapping the sole of the plane

Tape a length of emery paper to a smooth and flat surface, such as a glass plate or saw table. Reattach the handles and the frog to the body of the plane, then slide the sole along the emery paper, applying even pressure to keep the sole flat *(right)*. Continue lapping the sole until the metal on its bottom surface is uniformly bright and clean, indicating that the sole is level. Check the sole for square periodically.

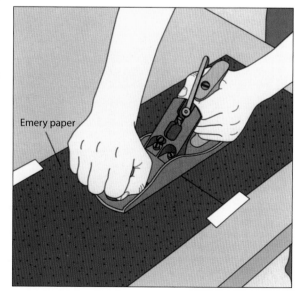

Emery paper

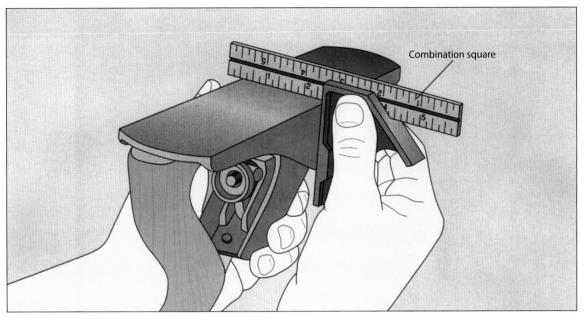

Combination square

Checking the sole for square

The bottom and sides of the plane's sole should be exactly at 90° to each other. Holding the plane in one hand, butt a combination square against the bottom and one side of the sole *(above)*. Repeat for the other side. The surfaces should be square both ways. If not, you will need to continue lapping the sole and the sides.

Sharpening a Plane Blade

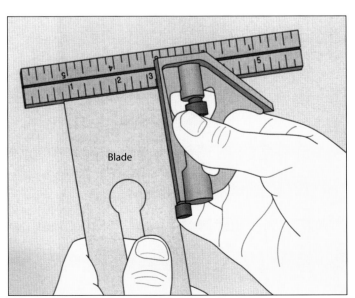

Blade

Checking the cutting edge for square

Use a combination square to determine whether the cutting edge of the plane blade is square to the sides *(left)*. If it is not, square the cutting edge on a bench grinder, making sure to adjust the grinder's tool rest at 90° to the wheel.

Maintaining Hand Tools

Back to **Basics**

41

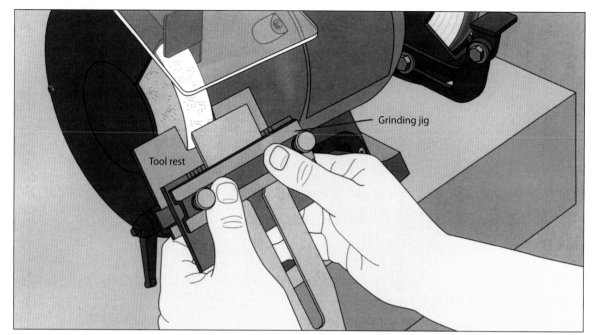

Grinding jig

Tool rest

Creating a hollow-ground bevel

Sharpening a plane blade involves three steps: creating a bevel on the blade's cutting edge, honing a microbevel on the first bevel, and removing the burr that results from the honing process. To create the first bevel, clamp the blade bevel-down in a commercial grinding jig and adjust the tool rest to create a 30° bevel. Holding the jig on the tool rest, advance it toward the wheel until the cutting edge makes contact *(above)*. Slide the blade side-to-side across the wheel, pressing lightly. Check the cutting edge periodically and stop grinding when the bevel forms.

Shop Tip

Grinding with a Sander

If you do not own a bench grinder, you can grind a plane blade on a belt sander. Install a 100-grit belt, mount the tool upside down in a stand, and secure the stand to a work surface. Turn on the sander and hold the beveled side of the blade on the belt at the appropriate angle.

Honing the microbevel

Once you sharpen the plane blade's cutting edge on a grinder, the result will be a hollow-ground bevel *(inset, left)*. If you did the job by hand on a sharpening stone, you will obtain a flat bevel *(inset, right)*. In either case, you need to hone a microbevel on the first bevel. Place a combination sharpening stone fine side up on a work surface. Screw cleats to the table against the stone to keep it from moving. For a hollow-ground bevel, clamp the blade in a commercial angle-setting honing guide with the bevel touching the stone. Saturate the stone with the appropriate lubricant and then, holding the honing guide, slide the blade back and forth from end to end along the sharpening surface *(right)*. Apply moderate pressure until a microbevel forms. If you are starting with a flat bevel, clamp the blade in a commercial angle-setting honing guide with the bevel touching the stone. Then raise the angle of the blade a few degrees and complete the operation as for a hollow-ground bevel.

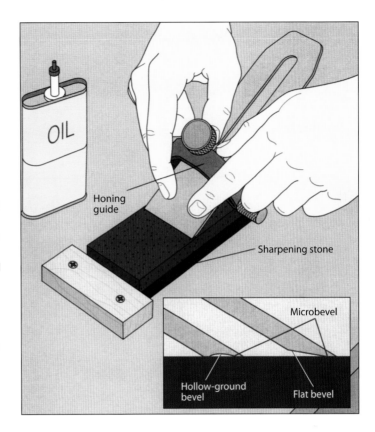

Honing guide

OIL

Sharpening stone

Microbevel

Hollow-ground bevel

Flat bevel

Lapping the burr

The honing process will create a thin ridge of metal, or burr, on the flat face of the blade. To remove the burr, saturate the fine side of the stone again. Holding the blade perfectly flat on the stone, bevel side up *(left)*, move it in a circular pattern until the flat side of the cutting edge is smooth.

Maintaining Hand Tools

Back to **Basics**

Testing the blade for sharpness

Clamp a softwood board to a work surface and, holding the blade bevel-side up in your hands, cut across the grain of the surface *(right)*. A sharp blade will cleanly slice a sliver of wood from the board without tearing the wood fibers.

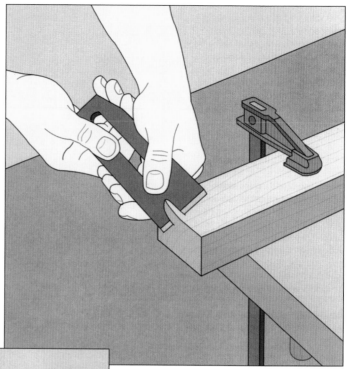

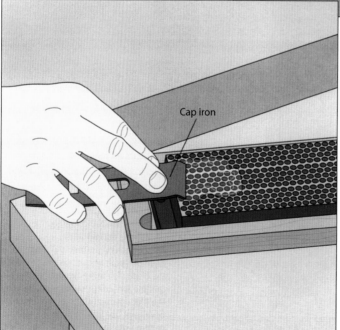

Cap iron

Honing the end of the cap iron

Secure a benchstone to your work surface; in the illustration at left, a diamond stone, which should be lubricated with water, is shown in its own box. Set the front portion of the cap iron that contacts the blade flat on the stone and slide it in a circular pattern on the surface *(left)*. Continue until the tip of the cap iron is perfectly flat. This will guarantee that wood chips will not become trapped between the iron and the blade once the two pieces are reassembled.

Assembling and Adjusting a Bench Plane

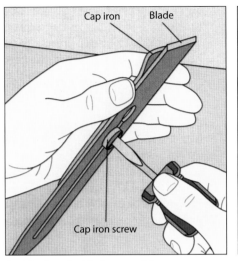

Cap iron — Blade

Cap iron screw

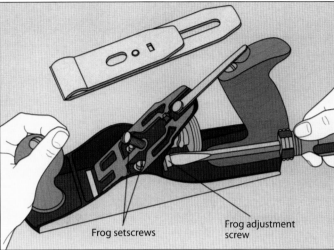

Frog setscrews

Frog adjustment screw

Positioning the blade assembly

Position the cap iron on the top face of the blade extending about $\frac{1}{16}$ inch beyond the end of the cap iron. Tighten the cap iron screw *(above, left)*. Then place the blade assembly—including the blade, cap iron, and lever cap—in position on the frog. The gap between the front edge of the blade and the front of the mouth should be between $\frac{1}{32}$ and $\frac{1}{16}$ inch. If the gap is too wide or narrow, remove the blade assembly and loosen both frog setscrews about $\frac{1}{4}$ turn. Then adjust the frog adjustment screw to set the proper gap *(above, right)*. Tighten the setscrews and reposition the blade assembly on the frog, securing it in place with the cap lock.

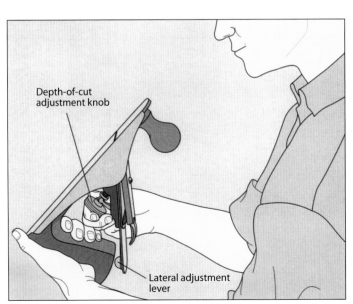

Depth-of-cut adjustment knob

Lateral adjustment lever

Centering the blade and adjusting the depth of cut

Holding the plane upside down, move the lateral adjustment lever until the cutting edge is parallel to the sole and centered in the mouth. To set the cutting depth, turn the depth-of-cut adjustment knob so the blade protrudes from the mouth *(left)*. About $\frac{1}{32}$ inch is desirable; less for highly figured woods. Confirm the setting with a test cut on a scrap board. The shavings should be paper-thin.

Scrapers

Properly honed, a hand or cabinet scraper is unsurpassed for smoothing and flattening a wood surface before finishing. For either type of scraper, sharpening is a four-step process, shown beginning on page 47. First, the edges of the scraper are filed square, then honed, and finally turned over into a burr and a hook *(page 48)*. You can produce the burr and the hook in two steps with a standard burnisher, like the one shown below, or create the hook in one operation with a variable burnisher *(photo, right*. The result is a cutting edge that should be capable of slicing paper-thin curls of wood from a workpiece.

Honing a hand scraper is simple work with the help of the variable burnisher shown above. The device features a carbide rod mounted within the wood body. A knob on the top adjusts the angle of the rod, providing precise control of the burnishing angle, while the jig is run back and forth over the cutting edge

Inventory of Scrapers and Accessories

Cabinet scraper
Twin handles offer greater control than a hand scraper.

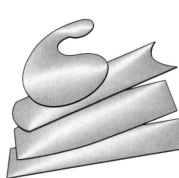

Hand scrapers
Steel blades are available in various shapes for smoothing curved or flat surfaces.

Burnisher
Forms the fine burr and hook on the cutting edge of a scraper after honing. Round models are usually used for curved scrapers and triangular models for rectangular scrapers; tri-burnisher shown combines round, rectangular, and oval burnishers in one tool.

Sharpening a Hand Scraper

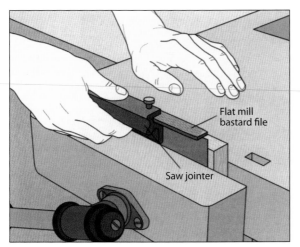

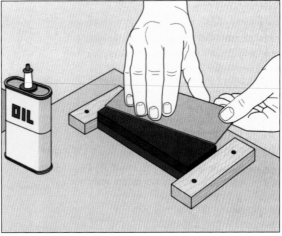

Filing the edges square

Secure the scraper in a vise, edge up, with a wood block on one side to keep it rigid. Clamp a mill bastard file in a commercial saw jointer and press the jointer firmly against one side of the scraper. Exert moderate pressure as you make several passes back and forth along the edge of the tool *(above)* until the existing hook disappears and the edge is flat. Turn the scraper over in the vise and repeat the process for the other edge.

Honing the edges

Secure a combination sharpening stone fine-side up on a work surface with cleats and lubricate it. Pressing the scraper flat on the stone, rub each face with a circular motion *(above)* until any roughness produced by filing disappears. Next, hold the scraper upright and slide the edges back and forth diagonally across the stone until they are smooth with sharp corners. To finish, again slide the face lightly over the stone to remove any burrs.

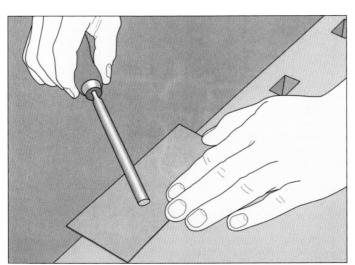

Burnishing the edges

Wipe a tiny amount of oil onto the edge of the scraper to reduce friction between the burnisher and the scraper. Start to form a hook on each cutting edge of the scraper by laying the scraper flat on a work surface with an edge extending off the table, then run the burnisher back and forth along the edge *(left)*, exerting strong downward pressure. Turn the scraper over and burnish the edge on the other face. Now burnish the other cutting edge the same way.

Maintaining Hand Tools

Back to **Basics**

47

Turning the hook

Secure the scraper edge up in the vise and wipe a little more oil onto its edge. Holding the burnisher level, make a few passes along the edge in one direction until the edge swells slightly. Apply moderate pressure to turn the edge outward on one side *(right)*. Then hold the burnisher so that the handle is 10° to 15° above the horizontal and continue to burnish until the edge turns over into a hook. To form a hook on the other side of the edge *(below)*, repeat the process with the scraper turned around in the vise. The greater the pressure you apply, the bigger the hook. Turn the scraper over in the vise and turn the hooks on the opposite edge.

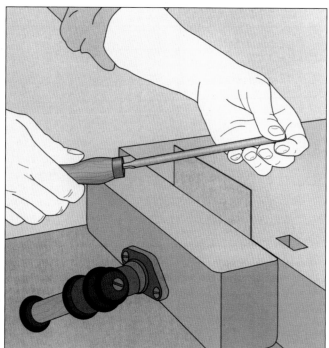

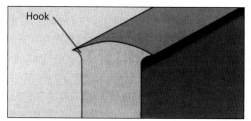

Hook

Sharpening a Cabinet Scraper

Filing the edge

Although its edge is beveled, a cabinet scraper is sharpened in much the same way as a hand scraper. Start by filing the bevel, then polish the bevel and turn over a hook. Remove the blade from the cabinet scraper by loosening the thumbscrews holding it in place. Clamp the blade beveled-edge up in a vise between two wood pads. Then run a bastard mill file along the bevel, using a combination square periodically to check that the angle remains at 45° *(right)*.

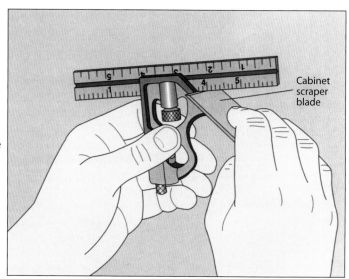

Cabinet scraper blade

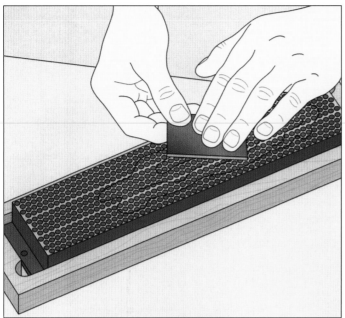

Polishing the bevel

Secure a sharpening stone to a work surface; in the illustration at left, a diamond stone is shown in a sharpening box. Lubricate the stone, then hold the scraper blade flat-side down and slide the blade in a circular pattern to remove any burr formed by filing. Next, turn the blade over so the bevel is flush on the stone and repeat to polish the bevel. A few passes should be sufficient. Use the combination square to help you maintain the bevel angle at 45°.

Burnishing the cutting edge

Hold the scraper blade bevel down on a work surface with the cutting edge overhanging the table. Wipe some oil on the edge and, holding a burnisher at a slight angle to the blade, pass the rod back and forth across its flat edge *(below)*. Apply strong downward pressure forming a hook on the cutting edge.

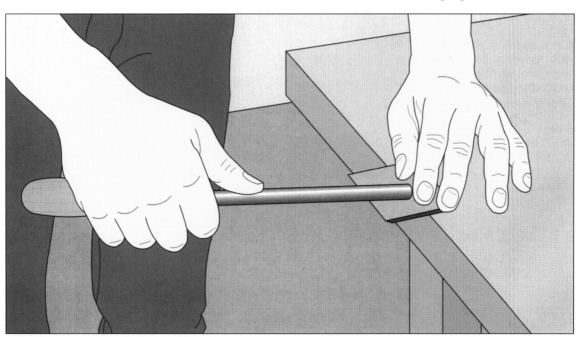

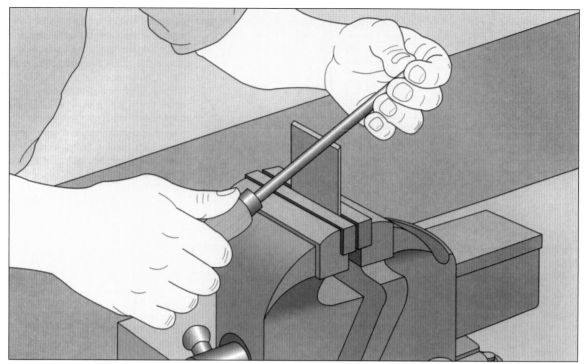

Forming the hook

Secure the blade bevel up in a machinist's vise and apply a little more oil on it. Holding the burnisher in both hands flush against the 45° bevel, pull the tool toward your body; maintain constant downward pressure *(above)*. Gradually tilt the handle of the burnisher until the rod is at angle of about 15° to the bevel. This will complete the hook on the cutting edge.

Shop Tip

Maintaining the correct burnishing angle

Holding a burnisher at the proper angle is the key to burnishing the bevel of a cabinet scraper. As a visual guide, use a protractor and a square to mark a line at a 45° angle on the wall facing you when you do the burnishing. Locate the mark at eye level directly in line with your vise. As you pass the burnisher along the bevel, try to keep the rod parallel with the line on the wall.

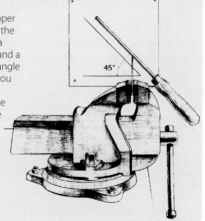

Roughing and Shaping Tools

The hand tools featured in this section of the chapter are as diverse as the individual tasks needed to work a standing tree into a piece of furniture. They range from rough to fine—axe to spokeshave, an implement most often used to whittle a workpiece to its final form.

For the sharpener, however, all these tools share one feature: They are single-bladed tools that rely on a correctly angled bevel to cut wood properly. The following pages will show you how to hone and polish each of the tools shown below. The first step in the process involves smoothing away defects and restoring the bevel on the blade, if the cutting edge requires it. This can be done on a bench grinder as you would a plane blade *(page 42)* or on a wet/dry grinder *(photo, right)*. To prolong blade life, grind only what is required to restore the edge. Also, be careful not to overheat the blade; this can destroy the temper of the metal. One advantage of the wet/dry grinder is that you do not have

A wet-dry grinder touches up an ax blade. To create a uniform bevel across the blade, it is important to hold the blade square to the grinding wheel and at a constant angle.

to interrupt the grinding periodically to cool the blade. The water-bathed wheel automatically takes care of this concern.

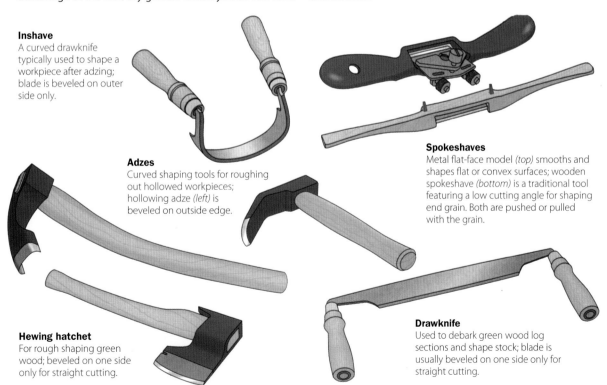

Inshave
A curved drawknife typically used to shape a workpiece after adzing; blade is beveled on outer side only.

Adzes
Curved shaping tools for roughing out hollowed workpieces; hollowing adze *(left)* is beveled on outside edge.

Spokeshaves
Metal flat-face model *(top)* smooths and shapes flat or convex surfaces; wooden spokeshave *(bottom)* is a traditional tool featuring a low cutting angle for shaping end grain. Both are pushed or pulled with the grain.

Hewing hatchet
For rough shaping green wood; beveled on one side only for straight cutting.

Drawknife
Used to debark green wood log sections and shape stock; blade is usually beveled on one side only for straight cutting.

51

Sharpening Spokeshaves

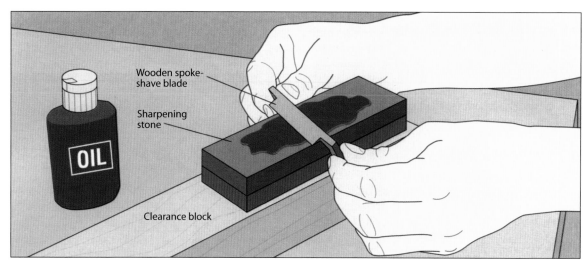

Wooden spoke-
shave blade

Sharpening
stone

OIL

Clearance block

Sharpening a wooden spokeshave blade

Remove the blade from the handle by pinching the tangs that protrude through the handle and pushing them downward. For sharpening, the blade is held upside down from its usual cutting position—that is, with the tangs facing down rather than up. To prevent the tangs from catching on your work surface during sharpening, set your sharpening stone atop a wood block to provide the necessary clearance. Holding the

blade by the tangs, set its bevel flat on the stone. Because the blade is longer than the width of the stone, hold the cutting edge diagonally as you slide the bevel back and forth on the stone. Repeat with the blade angled the other way. Repeat again with the blade held straight *(above)*. Once the sharpening is complete, turn the blade over and hone the flat side to remove the burr formed by the sharpening process.

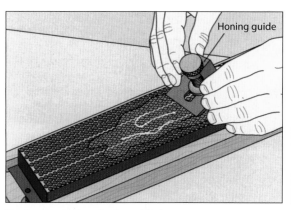

Honing guide

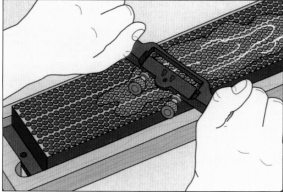

Honing a metal spokeshave blade

To remove the blade from the handle, loosen the screw in the middle of the handle. Set up a benchstone on a work surface; a water-lubricated diamond stone in a sharpening box is shown above. Install the blade in a commercial honing guide

(above, left) and hone the cutting edge as you would a plane blade *(page 43)*. To flatten the sole of a flat-soled spokeshave, pass the sole back and forth along a medium-grit benchstone *(above, right)*. Continue until the metal has uniform sheen.

Sharpening a Drawknife

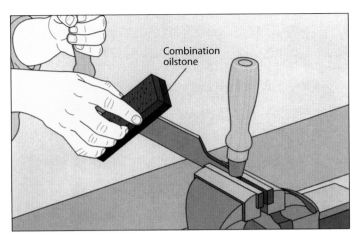

Combination oilstone

Honing a drawknife

Secure one handle of the drawknife in a machinist's vise with the blade level and the bevel facing up. Then lubricate a fine benchstone—in this case, a combination stone—and rub the stone along the length of the bevel, using a circular motion *(left)*. To hone a microbevel on the primary bevel, adjust the angle of the stone slightly. Finally, make a few passes on the flat side of the blade to remove any burr formed by sharpening.

Sharpening an Inshave

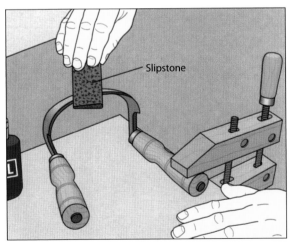

Slipstone

Sharpening an Adze

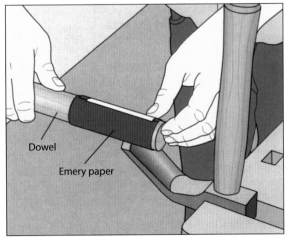

Dowel

Emery paper

Honing an inshave

Clamp the inshave to a work surface so the cutting edge is facing up, as shown above. Use a slipstone to hone the edge. Start with a rough-grit stone and progress to a finer one. Work with a circular motion until a uniform shine develops on the blade. Give the flat side of the blade a few strokes to remove any burr. Once the blade is sharp, polish the bevel with a leather strop and polishing compound *(page 37)*, finishing with a few passes on the flat side of the blade to remove the burr. If the inshave has a knife-edge—beveled on both sides—hone the other side.

Honing an adze

Secure the adze in a bench vise, as shown above. Wrap a sheet of emery paper around a dowel whose diameter closely matches the curve of the adze blade. Hone the cutting edge using a back-and-forth motion along the length of the bevel. Hone the flat side of the blade with a slipstone to remove any burr. If the adze has a knife-edge hone the other side.

Polishing the Blade

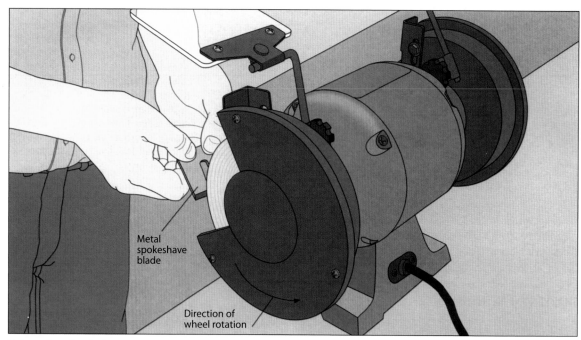

Metal
spokeshave
blade

Direction of
wheel rotation

Using a bench grinder
Once you have sharpened the blade of a
roughing or shaping tool, polish the bevel and
remove any burr formed by the process on
the felt wheel of a bench grinder. For a metal
spokeshave blade, impregnate the wheel with
polishing compound and place the bevel of the
blade on the trailing edge of the wheel *(above)*.
Move the blade side to side to expose the entire
bevel to the wheel. Buff the blade only enough
to remove the burr, using a light touch to avoid
rounding the edge. Run the whole length of the
bevel back and forth across the wheel to polish
it uniformly. Repeat on the flat side of the blade.
Test the cutting edge for sharpness on a piece of
softwood *(page 44)*.

Shop Tip

Choosing a durable ax handle
Despite the availability of a variety of
synthetic compounds, wooden-handled
axes remain popular. They are light and
strong, and feature a well-balanced feel.
The strength of the handle
depends on the orientation
of the grain to the ax head.
Choose an ax with a handle that
has the grain running parallel
to the cutting edge *(bottom)*;
handles with the grain running
perpendicular *(top)* to the face
tend to break more easily.

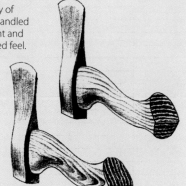

Braces and Bits

Electric drills have largely superseded hand tools for boring holes in the modern woodshop. Nevertheless, most woodworkers still keep braces and hand drills handy, because these tools have unique capabilities not readily duplicated by power tools, such as working in tight quarters or boring a hole to a precise depth.

Maintaining these hand tools is mainly a question of keeping their moving parts clean and sharpening their bits. To clean a brace, unscrew the chuck shell and remove the jaws, as shown at right. Use the same cleaning procedure as you would for the parts of a bench plane *(page 40)*. The remaining pages of this chapter describe how to sharpen auger and spoon bits.

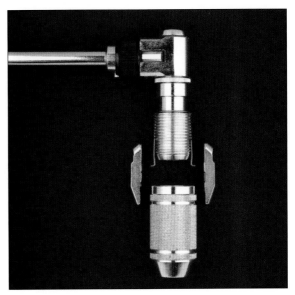

Cleaning the chuck is an essential element of maintaining a brace. The exploded view of a brace chuck in the photo at right shows the parts that require cleaning: the shell and the two-piece jaw.

Anatomy of Auger and Spoon Bits

Cutting edge, or lip

Spur

Auger bit
The cutting edge—or lip—bites, pulls, and guides the bit into the workpiece; the spurs score the outline of the hole so that the lip does not tear the wood fibers.

Bit nose

Spoon bit
This traditional chair maker's bit features a slightly pointed nose that is self-guiding as the sides of the bit bore a straight-sided hole.

Back to **Basics**

Sharpening an Auger Bit

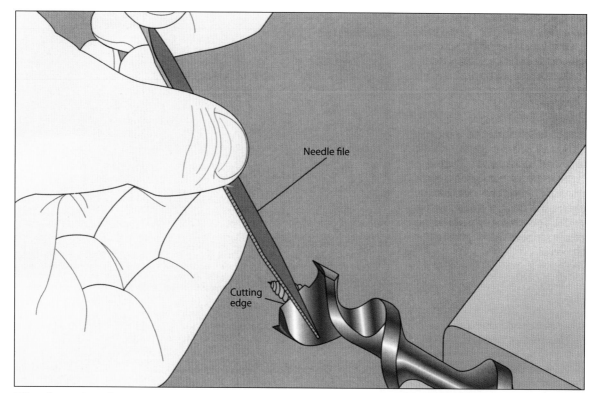

Needle file

Cutting edge

Filing the cutting edge

Secure the bit in a bench vise, then use a needle file to sharpen the cutting edge. (You can also use a specialized auger bit file for the job.) Hold the file on the leading edge and make a few strokes along the surface. Repeat with the other cutting edge.

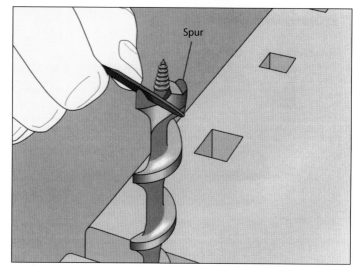

Spur

Filing the spur

Position the bit upright in the vise. Holding the file flush against the inside edge of one spur, make several strokes across the surface *(right)* until you produce an even shine on the spur. Repeat with the other spur.

Removing burrs from the spurs

Holding a very fine diamond hone on a work surface, slide the outside edge of one of the bit spurs on the stone to remove any burr formed by sharpening *(right)*. (You can also use a piece of very fine emery cloth.) Work with a light touch and use only enough strokes to remove the burr, or you risk reducing the bit diameter. Repeat with the other spur.

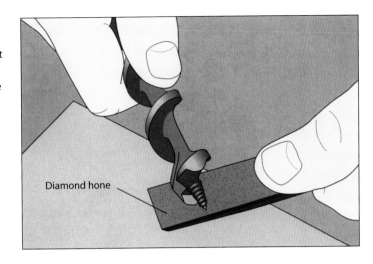

Diamond hone

Sharpening a Spoon Bit

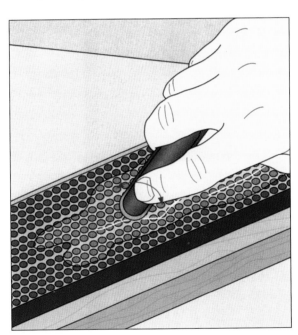

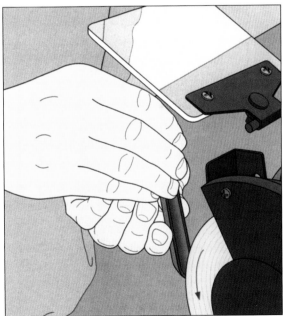

Sharpening a spoon bit

Spoon bits can be sharpened easily on a benchstone. In the illustration above, at left, a diamond stone in its own sharpening box is shown. Holding the outside of the bit's nose on the stone, rock the bit across the surface with a semicircular motion. Hold the bit at the same angle throughout to ensure that the nose is honed uniformly. Once the sharpening is completed, polish both sides of the nose on the felt wheel of a bench grinder. Impregnate the wheel with polishing compound and, holding the bit vertically, lightly touch the front of the nose to the wheel *(above, right)*. Repeat with the back side.

Sharpening Blades and Bits

Like any cutting or shaping tool, a power tool with a dull blade or bit cannot perform well. A dull drill bit will tend to skate off a workpiece, rather than biting cleanly into the wood. A saw blade or router bit with blunted cutting edges may burn stock. And wood that is surfaced by a jointer or planer with unsharpened knives may be difficult to glue up or finish.

In addition to cutting and shaping properly, well-sharpened blades and bits offer other benefits, including reduced wear and tear on motors, less operator fatigue, and longer life for the blades and bits themselves. Manufacturers of power tool blades and bits generally recommend sending their products to a professional sharpening service. However, the job can often be done in the workshop. This chapter will show you how to sharpen a wide variety of power tool blades and bits, from router bits and shaper cutters *(page 62)* to jointer and planer knives *(page 79)*. In a pinch, even a broken band saw blade can be soldered together *(page 76)*.

Still, there are times when you should turn to a professional, particularly if blades and bits have chipped edges or have lost their

temper as a result of overgrinding. Some router bits also must be precisely balanced, something that is difficult to achieve in the shop. As a rule of thumb, it is a good idea to send out your bits and blades to a sharpening service periodically, or every second time they need a major sharpening. Once you have sharpened an edge properly, it should last for a long time—the occasional honing is all that it takes to maintain it.

The pages that follow cover the basic techniques for sharpening power tool blades and bits in the shop. With a little practice and the right accessories, you can keep the cutting edges of your blades and bits razor-sharp. But remember that a keen edge always starts with the quality of the steel itself; for long life and ease of sharpening, always choose bits and blades made from the best steel.

Designed to replace the metal guide blocks supplied with most band saws, heat-resistant guide blocks can help prolong blade life. Made from a graphite-impregnated resin that is its own lubricant, these nonmetallic blocks last longer than metal blocks and can be set closer to the blade, allowing more accurate and controlled cuts.

A twist bit is sharpened on a bench grinder with the help of a commercial grinding jig that holds the bit at the proper angle. Originally designed for the metal-working industry, twist bits took their place in woodworking as the use of power tools grew. They need periodic sharpening to bore holes cleanly and accurately.

A Gallery of Blades and Bits

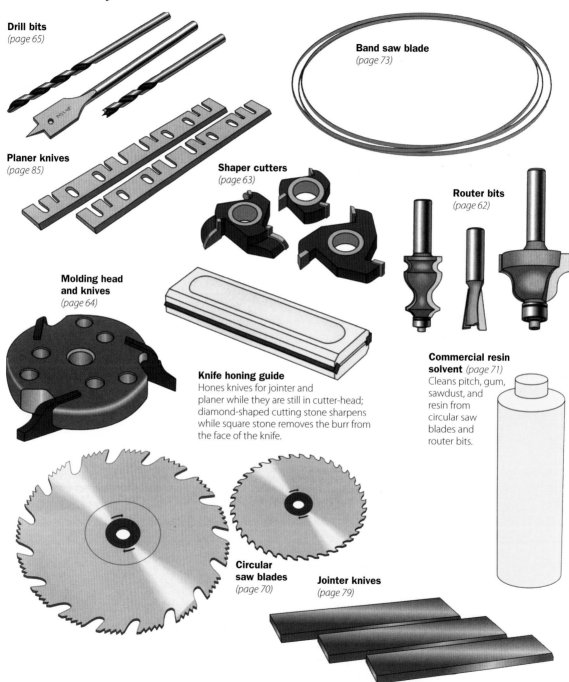

Drill bits
(page 65)

Band saw blade
(page 73)

Planer knives
(page 85)

Shaper cutters
(page 63)

Router bits
(page 62)

**Molding head
and knives**
(page 64)

Knife honing guide
Hones knives for jointer and
planer while they are still in cutter-head;
diamond-shaped cutting stone sharpens
while square stone removes the burr from
the face of the knife.

**Commercial resin
solvent** *(page 71)*
Cleans pitch, gum,
sawdust, and
resin from
circular saw
blades and
router bits.

**Circular
saw blades**
(page 70)

Jointer knives
(page 79)

Tools and Accessories for Sharpening

Drill bit grinding attachment *(page 58)*
Holds ⅛- to ¾-inch-diameter twist bits for sharpening; mounted to work surface and used with a bench grinder.

Router bit sharpener
A boron-carbide stone used to sharpen carbon steel, high-speed steel, and carbide-tipped router bits; gives a finer finish than diamond files of equal grit. Handle features magnifying lens for checking sharpness.

Drill bit-sharpening jig *(page 66)*
Powered by an electric drill, this jig sharpens high-speed steel twist bits and carbide masonry bits up to ½ inch in diameter; holder secures bit at proper depth and angle against sharpening stone inside jig.

Circular saw blade-setting jig *(page 72)*
Clamped in bench vise to joint and set the teeth of circular saws up to 12 inches in diameter. Blade is locked in jig and rotated against file to joint teeth; teeth are set by tapping them with a hammer against mandrel.

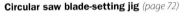

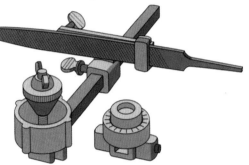

Knife-setting jigs *(page 85)*
Magnetic jig used to hold jointer or planer knives at the correct height for installation in the machine. Jigs for planer *(below)* are used in pairs for knives up to 20 inches long; jig for jointer *(right)* sets knives up to 8 inches in length, and can be extended with a third bar for knives up to 14 inches long.

Jointer/planer-knife sharpening jig *(page 82)*
Used to sharpen jointer and planer knives; knife is clamped in jig and rear screw adjusts to hold knife at proper angle against a bench stone.

Circular saw blade-sharpening jig *(page 72)*
Mounted on workbench to sharpen circular saw blades after grinding and setting; blade is held in jig while taper file is drawn across the teeth at the proper pitch and angle.

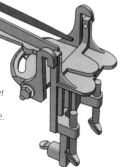

Router Bits and Shaper Cutters

Secured in a bench vise, one of the cutting edges of a shaper cutter receives its final sharpening with a fine diamond hone. The process is a two-step operation, beginning with a medium hone *(far left)*. Because they operate at high speeds, dull router bits and shaper cutters overheat quickly. Cutters that are properly sharpened make smoother, more accurate cuts.

Sharpening a Non-Piloted Router Bit

Sharpening the inside faces

Clean any pitch, gum, or sawdust off the bit with a commercial resin solvent *(page 71)*, then use a ceramic or diamond sharpening file to hone the inside faces of the bit's cutting edges. A coarse-grit file is best if a lot of material needs to be removed; use a finer-grit file for a light touch-up. Holding the inside face of one cutting edge flat against the abrasive surface, rub it back and forth *(right)*. Repeat with the other cutting edge. Hone both inside faces equally to maintain the balance of the bit. Take care not to file the bevel behind the cutting edge.

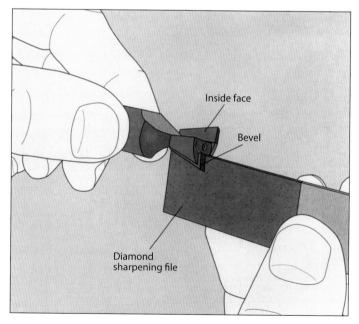

Inside face

Bevel

Diamond sharpening file

Sharpening a Piloted Router Bit

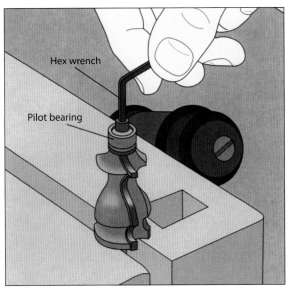

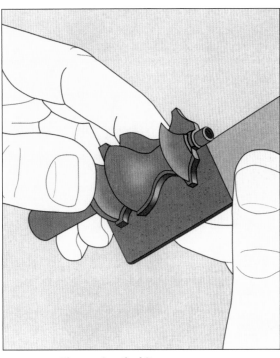

Removing the pilot bearing
Before you can sharpen a piloted router bit, you need to remove the pilot bearing. Use a hex wrench to loosen the bearing *(above)*.

Sharpening the bit
Sharpen the bit with a ceramic or diamond sharpening file as you would a non-piloted bit *(page 62);* then re-install the bearing with the hex wrench. If the bearing does not rotate smoothly, spray a little bearing lubricant on it. If it is worn out or damaged, replace it.

Shop Tip

A storage rack for shaper cutters
Shaper cutters are often sold in cumbersome packaging that can contribute to clutter. Organize your shaper bits with a shop-made storage rack like the one shown here. The rack will keep the cutters visible and accessible. Drill a series of holes in a board and glue dowels in the holes to hold the cutters. To prevent the cutting edges from nicking each other, use your largest-diameter cutter as a guide to spacing the dowel holes. If you plan to hang the rack on a wall, bore the holes at a slight angle so that the cutters will not slip off the dowels.

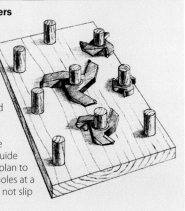

Molding Knives

Sharpening Molding Knives

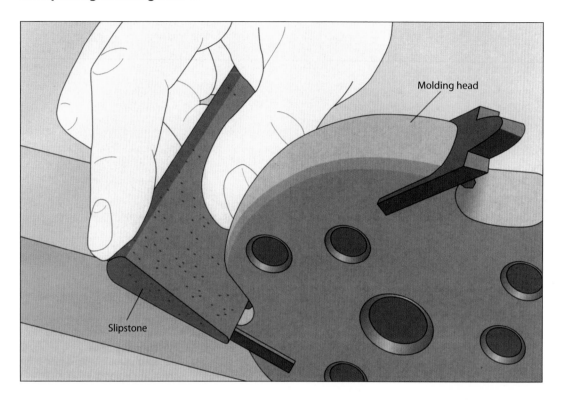

Molding head

Slipstone

Sharpening molding knives

The cutting edges of table saw or radial arm saw molding knives are easy to touch up or sharpen while they are mounted in the molding head. Clamp the head in a bench vise with one of the knives clear of the bench, then use a slipstone *(above)* to hone its inside face as you would a router bit *(page 62)*. Reposition the head in the vise to hone the remaining knives. Use the same number of strokes to hone each knife so that you remove an equal amount of metal from them all, and maintain their identical shapes and weights. An alternative method involves removing the knives with a hex wrench *(right)* and sharpening them on a flat oilstone.

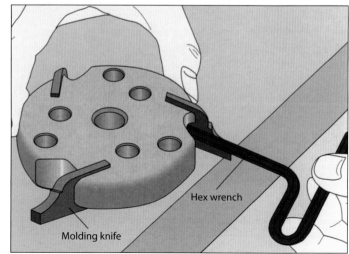

Hex wrench

Molding knife

64

Drill Bits

Sharpening Twist Bits

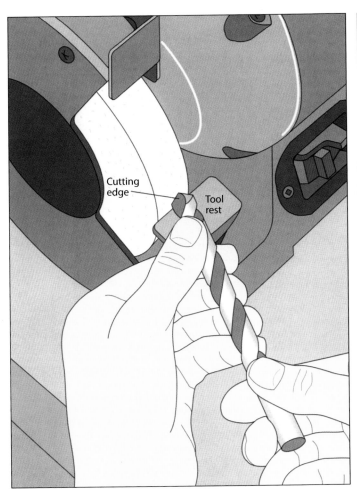

Cutting edge

Tool rest

Using a bench grinder

Holding the bit between the index finger and thumb of one hand, set it on the grinder's tool rest and advance it toward the wheel until your index finger contacts the tool rest. Tilt the shaft of the bit down and to the left so that one of the cutting edges, or lips, is square to the wheel (*above*). Rotate the bit clockwise to grind the lip evenly. Periodically check the angle of the cutting edge, as shown in the photo at right, and try to maintain the angle at about 60°. Repeat for the second cutting edge. To keep bits sharp, use them at the speed recommended by the manufacturer. Wipe them occasionally with oil to prevent rust.

To bore clean holes, the cutting edges of twist bits should be angled at about 60°. As you sharpen a bit, periodically check the angle with a protractor. Butt one of the cutting edges against the base of the protractor and swivel the arm flush against the side of the bit.

65

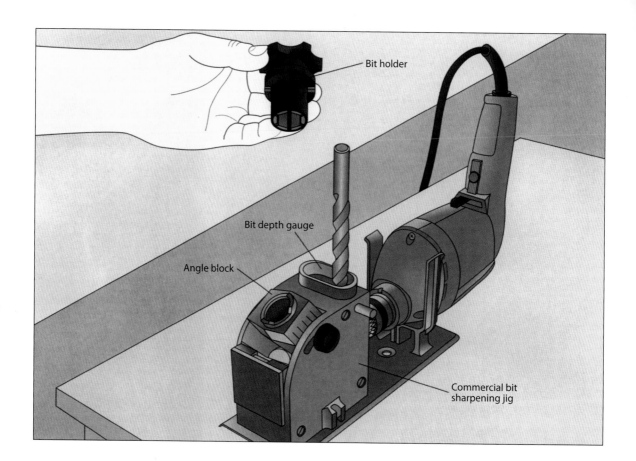

Bit holder

Bit depth gauge

Angle block

Commercial bit
sharpening jig

Using a commercial jig

Set up the jig following the manufacturer's
instructions. For the model shown, secure an
electric drill to the jig; the drill will rotate the
sharpening stone inside the device. Adjust the
angle block to the appropriate angle for the bit
to be sharpened and insert the bit in the depth
gauge. The gauge will enable you to secure the
bit at the correct height in the holder. Fit the bit
holder over the bit *(above)* and then use it to
remove the bit from the gauge. Now secure the
bit and holder to the angle block. Turn on the
drill and, holding it steady, slowly rotate the bit
holder a full 360° against the stone inside the jig
(right). Apply light pressure; too much force will
overheat the bit.

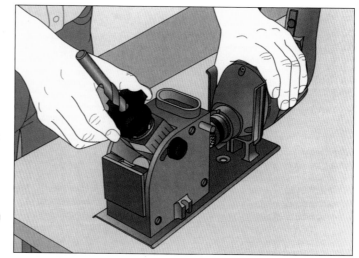

Sharpening Forstner Bits

Grinding the inside bevel

To touch up a Forstner bit, true the top edge of the bit's rim with a file, removing any nicks. If the beveled edges of the cutting spurs inside the rim are uneven, grind them using an electric drill fitted with a rotary grinding attachment. Secure the bit in a bench vise as shown and grind the edges until they are all uniform *(right)*.

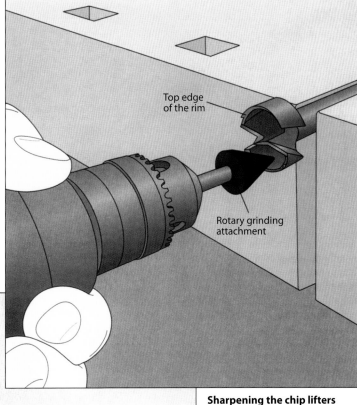

Top edge of the rim

Rotary grinding attachment

Sharpening the chip lifters

Use a single-cut mill bastard file to lightly file the inside faces of the cutters. Hold the file flat against one of the cutters—also known as chip lifters—and make a few strokes along the surface *(left)*. Repeat with the other cutter. Finish the job by honing the beveled edges inside the rim with a slipstone.

Chip lifter

Honing Multi-Spur Bits

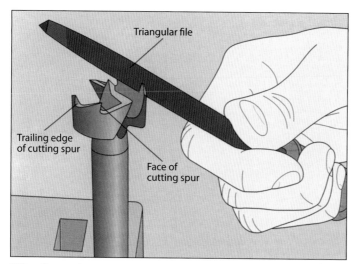

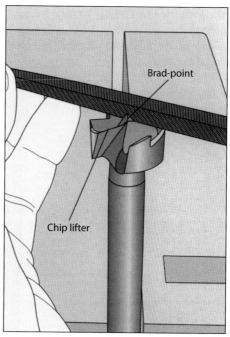

Filing the cutting spurs
Secure the bit upright in a bench vise and use a triangular file to hone the leading edge, or face, of each spur *(above)*. File with each push stroke, towards the bit's brad point, tilting the handle of the file down slightly. Then file the trailing edge, or back, of each spur the same way. File all the spurs by the same amount so that they remain at the same height. Make sure you do not over-file the cutting spurs; they are designed to be 1/32 inch longer than the chip lifters.

Filing the brad point
File the chip lifters as you would those of a Forstner bit *(page 67)*. Then, file the brad-point until it is sharp *(above)*.

Sharpening Brad-Point Bits

Filing the chip lifters
Clamp the bit upright in a bench vise and file the inside faces of the two chip lifters as you would those of a Forstner bit *(page 67)*. For a brad-point bit, however, use a triangular needle file *(right)*, honing until each cutting edge is sharp and each chip lifter is flat.

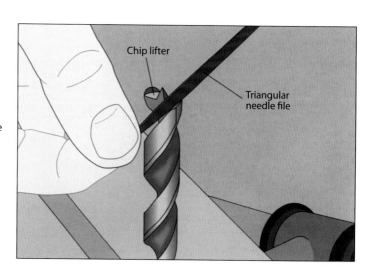

Filing the cutting spurs
Use the needle file to hone the inside faces of the bit's two cutting spurs. Hold the tool with both hands and file towards the brad-point until each spur is sharp *(right)*.

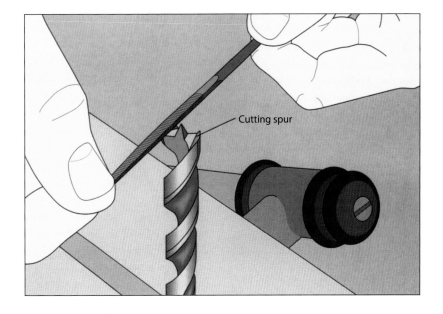

Cutting spur

Honing Spade Bits

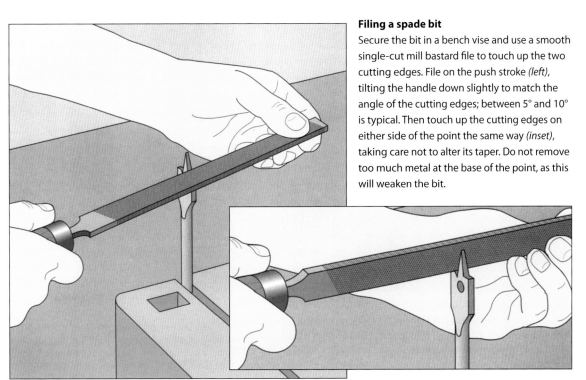

Filing a spade bit
Secure the bit in a bench vise and use a smooth single-cut mill bastard file to touch up the two cutting edges. File on the push stroke *(left)*, tilting the handle down slightly to match the angle of the cutting edges; between 5° and 10° is typical. Then touch up the cutting edges on either side of the point the same way *(inset)*, taking care not to alter its taper. Do not remove too much metal at the base of the point, as this will weaken the bit.

Circular Saw Blades

Changing Table Saw Blades

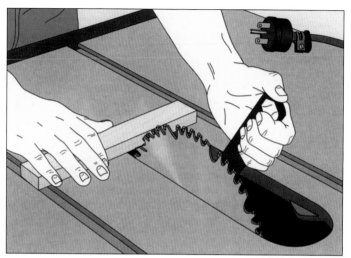

Removing a blade

Working at the front of the table, unplug the machine, remove the insert, and wedge a piece of scrap wood under a blade tooth to prevent the blade from turning. Use the wrench supplied with the saw to loosen the arbor nut *(left)*. (Most table saw arbors have reverse threads; the nut is loosened in a clockwise direction.) Finish loosening the nut by hand, making sure that it does not fall into the machine. Carefully lift the blade and washer off the arbor. Carbide-tipped blades are best sharpened professionally; but high-speed steel models can be sharpened in the shop *(page 72)*. A worn or damaged blade should be discarded and replaced.

The commercial blade carrier shown above is a handy storage device that will protect your circular saw blades from damage and make it easier to transport them. This model accommodates up to ten 10-inch blades.

Installing a blade

Slide the blade onto the arbor with its teeth pointing in the direction of blade rotation (toward the front of the table). Insert the flange and nut and start tightening by hand. To finish tightening, grip the saw blade with a rag and use the wrench supplied with the saw *(above)*. Do not use a piece of wood as a wedge, as this could result in overtightening the nut.

Changing Portable Circular Saw Blades

Removing a portable circular saw blade
Set the saw on its side on a work surface with the blade housing facing up. Retract the lower blade guard and, gripping the blade with a rag, loosen the arbor nut with the wrench supplied with the saw *(right)*. Remove the nut and the outer washer, then slide the blade from the arbor. As with table saw blades, carbide-tipped blades should be sent out for sharpening, but high-speed steel types can be sharpened in the shop. To install a blade, place it on the arbor with its teeth pointing in the direction of blade rotation. Install the washer and the nut, and tighten them by hand. Holding the blade with the rag, use the wrench to give the nut an additional quarter turn. Do not overtighten.

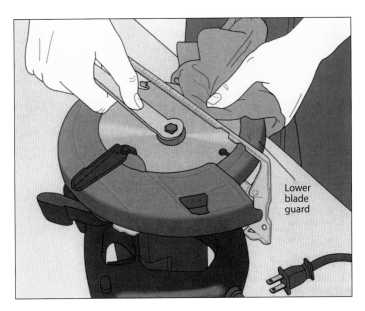

Lower blade guard

Cleaning Circular Saw Blades

Soaking the blade
Clean the blade using a commercial resin solvent. (Commercial oven cleaner, turpentine, or a solution of hot water with ammonia can also be used.) For stubborn pitch and gum deposits, soak the blade in the cleaning agent in a shallow pan and use a brass-bristled brush to clean the teeth *(left)*.

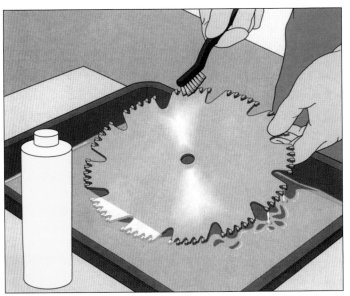

Sharpening Circular Saw Blades

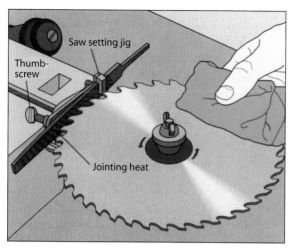

Jointing the teeth

To sharpen the teeth of a circular saw blade, install the blade in a commercial saw-setting jig following the manufacturer's instructions. For the model shown, the blade teeth should be pointing counterclockwise. Install the jointing head on the jig, butting its file up against the saw teeth. Then tighten the thumbscrew until the teeth drag against the file. To joint the teeth so they are all the same length, clamp the jig in a bench vise and rotate the blade against the file clockwise *(above)*. After each rotation, tighten the thumbscrew slightly and repeat until the tip of each tooth has been filed flat.

Setting the teeth

Remove the jointing head from the jig and install the setting head. Also remove the jig from the vise and set it on the benchtop. Adjust the head for the appropriate amount of set, or bend. Using a pin punch and ball-peen hammer, lightly strike every second tooth against the setting head *(above)*. Remove the blade and reverse the position of the setting head. Reinstall the blade with the teeth pointing in the opposite direction, and repeat for the teeth you skipped, again striking every second tooth.

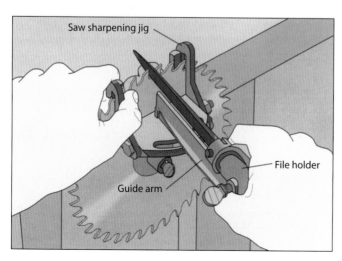

Sharpening the teeth

Once the saw teeth have been jointed and set, file them using a commercial saw-sharpening jig. Mount the jig to a workbench and install the blade loosely on the jig so the blade turns. Following the manufacturer's instructions, rotate the triangular file in the file holder and adjust the guide arm to match the required pitch and angle of the saw teeth. Starting with a tooth that is pointing to the right, file the cutting edge by sliding the file holder along the top of the jig *(left)*. Rotate the blade counterclockwise, skipping one tooth, and repeat. Sharpen all the right-pointing teeth the same way. Adjust the triangular file and the guide arm to work on the left-pointing teeth and repeat, sharpening all the teeth you skipped.

Band Saw Blades

Secured between two wood blocks in a bench vise, the teeth of a band saw blade are sharpened with a triangular file. Band saw blades can also be honed while they are installed on the machine. The teeth should be sharpened periodically and set after every three to five sharpenings. In fact, a properly honed and set band saw blade will perform better than a brand new one.

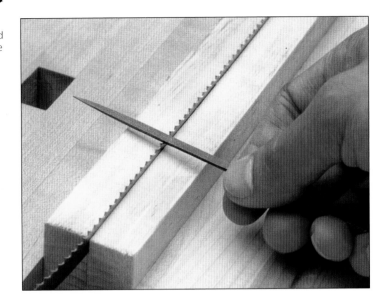

Sharpening a Band Saw Blade

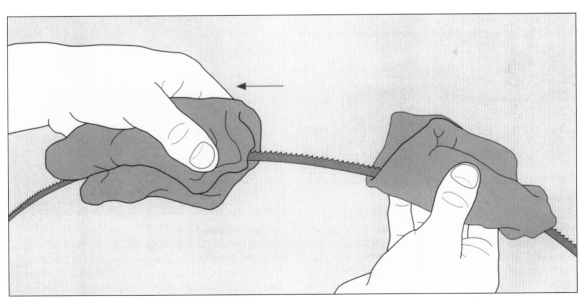

Cleaning the blade

Before sharpening a band saw blade, remove sawdust and wood chips from it. Make sure you release the blade tension first before slipping the blade off the wheels. Then, holding the blade between two clean rags (above), pull it away in the direction opposite its normal rotation to avoid snagging the cutting edges in the material.

Installing the blade for sharpening

You can sharpen a band saw blade either on a bench vise *(photo, page 73)* or on the machine. To install the blade on the band saw for sharpening, mount it with the teeth pointing in the direction opposite their cutting position— that is, facing up instead of down. Turn the blade inside out and guide it through the table slot *(right)*, holding it with the teeth facing you and pointing up. Slip the blade between the guide blocks and in the throat column slot, then center it on the wheels. Make sure the blade guide assembly is raised as high above the table as it will go.

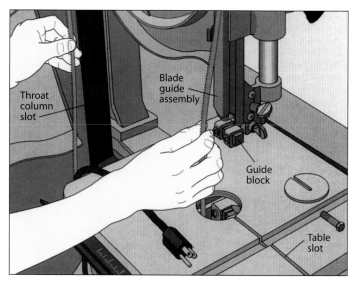

Setting the blade

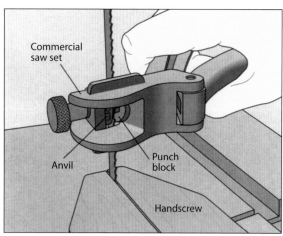

If the teeth need to be set, adjust a commercial saw set to the same number of teeth per inch as the band saw blade. Secure the blade in a handscrew and clamp the handscrew to the saw table. Starting at the handscrew-end of the blade, position the first tooth that is bent to the right between the anvil and punch block of the saw set and squeeze the handle to set the tooth *(above)*. Work your way up to the guide assembly, setting all the teeth that are bent to the right. Then turn the saw set over and repeat for the leftward-bent teeth. Continue setting all the blade teeth section by section. To ensure you do not omit any teeth, mark each section you work on with chalk.

Sharpening the blade

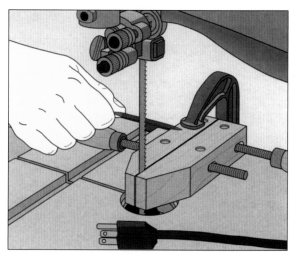

Sharpen the teeth the same way you set them, working on one blade section at a time. Hold a triangular file at a 90° angle to the blade and sharpen each tooth that is set to the right, guiding the file in the same direction that the tooth is set *(above)*. Then sharpen the leftward-bent teeth the same way. Use the same number of strokes on each tooth. Once all the teeth have been sharpened, remove the blade, turn it inside out and reinstall it for cutting, with the teeth pointing down. Tension and track the blade.

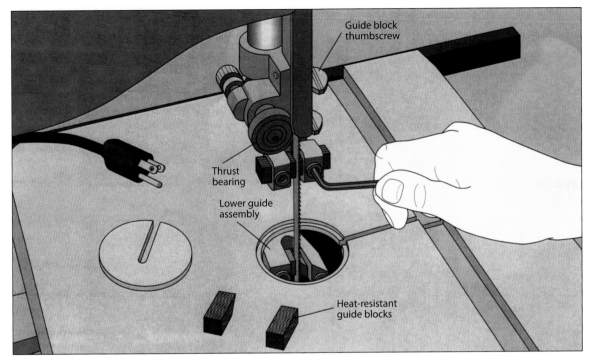

Guide block
thumbscrew

Thrust
bearing

Lower guide
assembly

Heat-resistant
guide blocks

Installing heat-resistant guide blocks

Replacing your band saw's standard guide blocks with heat-resistant blocks will lengthen blade life and promote more accurate and controlled cuts. Remove the original blocks by using a hex wrench to loosen the setscrews securing them to the upper guide assembly *(above)*. Slip out the old blocks and insert the replacements. Pinch the blocks together with your thumb and index finger until they almost touch the blade. (You can also use a slip of paper to set the space between the guide blocks and the blade). Tighten the setscrews. The front edges of the guide blocks should be just behind the blade gullets. To reposition the blocks, loosen their thumbscrew and turn their adjustment knob to advance or retract the blocks. Tighten the thumbscrew and repeat the process for the guide assembly located below the table.

Shop Tip

Rounding a band saw blade

To help prevent a new band saw blade from binding in the kerf of curved cut, use a silicon-carbide stone without oil to round its back edge, as shown here. Attach the stone to a shop-made handle. Tension and track the blade, then turn on the saw. Wearing safety goggles, hold the stone against the back of the blade and slowly pivot the stone. Turn off the saw after a few minutes. In addition to rounding the back of the blade, the stone will smooth any bumps where the blade ends are welded together.

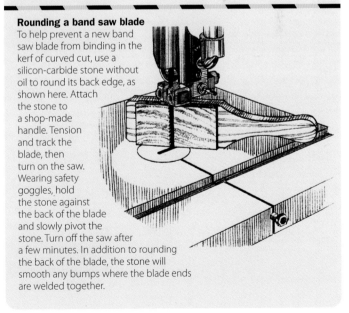

75

Repairing a Broken Band Saw Blade

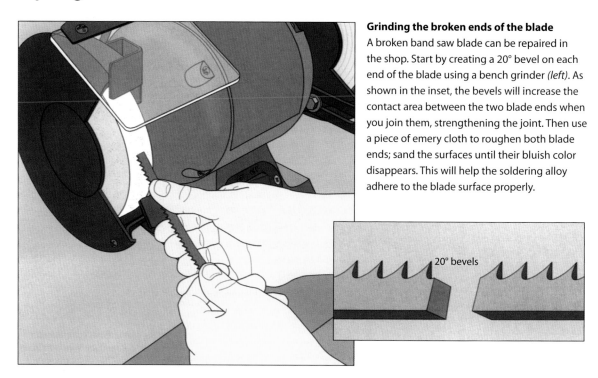

Grinding the broken ends of the blade
A broken band saw blade can be repaired in the shop. Start by creating a 20° bevel on each end of the blade using a bench grinder *(left)*. As shown in the inset, the bevels will increase the contact area between the two blade ends when you join them, strengthening the joint. Then use a piece of emery cloth to roughen both blade ends; sand the surfaces until their bluish color disappears. This will help the soldering alloy adhere to the blade surface properly.

20° bevels

Setting up the blade in the soldering jig
Secure a commercial soldering jig in a machinist's vise. Next, use a brush to spread flux on the beveled ends of the blade and ½ inch in from each end. Position the blade in the jig so the two beveled ends are in contact *(right)*. Make sure the blade is tight and straight in the jig.

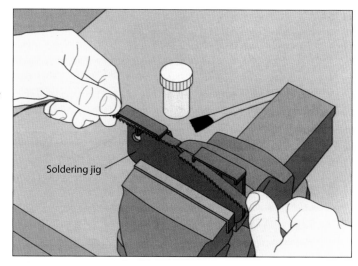

Soldering jig

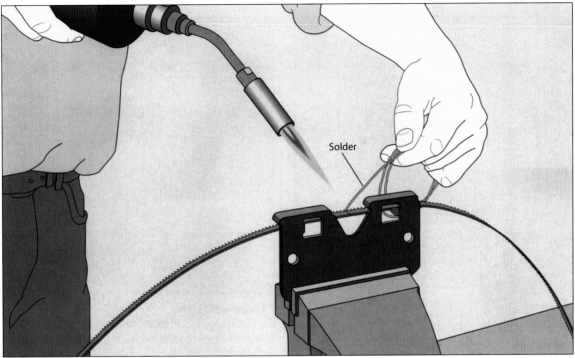

Soldering the blade ends

Heat the joint with a propane torch, then unroll a length of the solder and touch the tip to the joint—not to the flame. Continue heating the joint *(above)* until the solder covers the joint completely. Turn off the torch and let the joint cool.

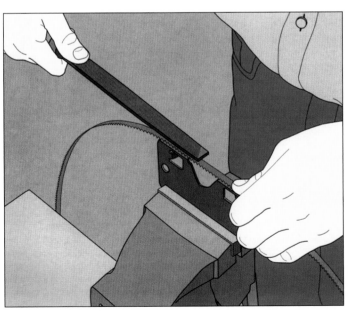

Filing the joint

Once the joint has cooled, remove the blade from the jig and wash off the flux with warm water. If there is an excess of solder on the blade, file it off carefully with a single-cut bastard mill file *(left)* until the joint is no thicker than the rest of the blade. If the joint separates, reheat it to melt the solder, pull it apart, and try again.

Folding and Storing a Band Saw Blade

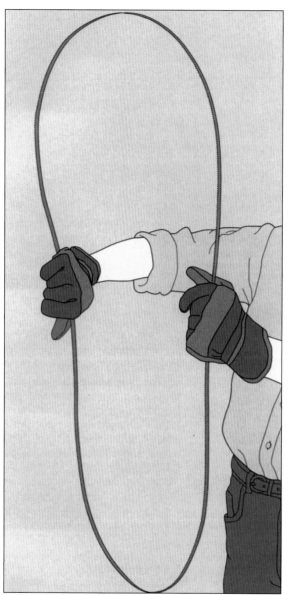

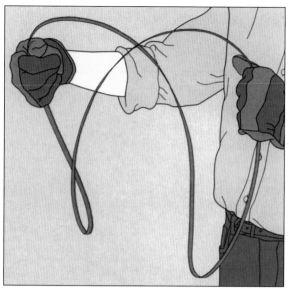

Twisting the blade

Pressing your right thumb firmly against the blade, twist it by pivoting your right hand upward. The blade will begin to form two loops *(above)*.

Coiling the blade

Without releasing the blade, keep rotating it in the same direction while pivoting your left hand in the opposite direction. The blade will coil again, forming a third loop *(above)*. Secure the blade with string, pipe cleaners, or plastic twist ties.

Holding the blade

Before storing a band saw blade, remove any rust from it with steel wool and wipe it with an oily rag. Then, wearing safety goggles and gloves, grasp with the teeth facing away; point your left thumb up and your right thumb down *(above)*.

Jointer and Planer Knives

A pair of magnetic jigs holds a planer knife at the correct height in the cutter-head, allowing the knife to be fixed in place accurately. Such jigs take the guesswork out of the trickiest phase of sharpening planer knives—installing them properly. Periodic sharpening of planer knives is essential. Stock that is surfaced by dull knives is difficult to glue and does not accept finishes well. A similar jig is available for setting jointer knives.

Honing Jointer Knives

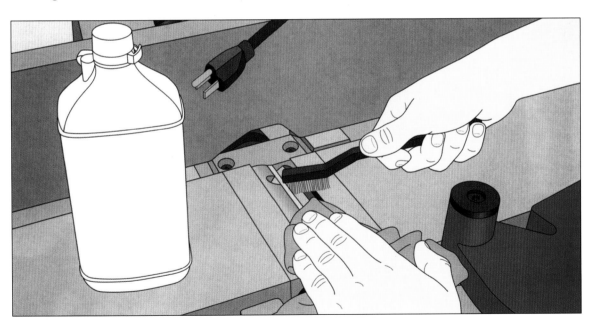

Cleaning the knives

Jointer knives can be honed while they are in the cutter-head. Start by cleaning them. Shift the fence away from the tables and move the guard out of the way. Making sure the jointer is unplugged, rotate the cutterhead with a stick until one of the knives is at the highest point in its rotation. Then, holding the cutterhead steady with one hand protected by a rag, use a small brass-bristled brush soaked in solvent to clean the knife *(above)*. Repeat for the other knives.

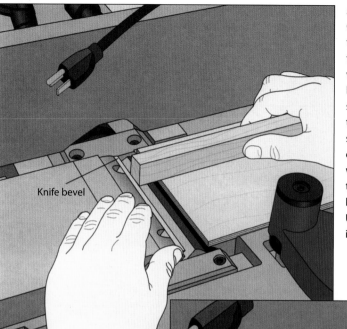

Knife bevel

Aligning the infeed table with the knives

Cut a piece of ¼-inch plywood to the width of the jointer's infeed table and secure it to the table with double-faced tape. The plywood will protect the table from scratches when you hone the knives. Next, adjust the infeed table so that the beveled edge of the knives is at the same level as the top of the plywood. Set a straight board on the plywood and across the cutterhead and, holding the cutterhead steady with the beveled edge of one knife parallel to the table, lower the infeed table until the bottom of the board contacts the bevel *(left)*. Use a wood shim to wedge the cutterhead in place.

Honing the knives

Slide a combination stone evenly across the beveled edge of the knife *(right)*. Move the stone with a side-to-side motion until the bevel is flat and sharp, avoiding contact with the cutterhead. Repeat the process to hone the remaining knives.

Combination stone

Shim

Sharpening Jointer Knives

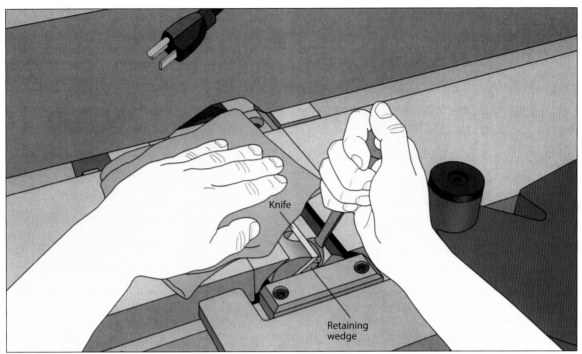

Knife

Retaining
wedge

Shop Tip

Shifting knives for longer life
To prolong the life of a set of jointer knives that have been nicked, loosen the lock screws securing one knife and slide the knife about ⅟₁₆ inch in either direction. Tighten the lock screws and carefully rotate the cutterhead by hand to ensure that the knife turns freely. Shifting a knife to one side moves its damaged segment out of alignment with the damage on the other knives, enabling the set to continue cutting smoothly.

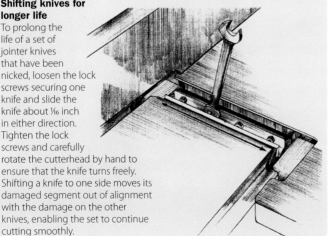

Removing the knives
To give jointer knives a full-fledged sharpening, remove them from the cutterhead. Unplug the machine, shift the fence away from the tables, and move the guard out of the way. Use a small wood scrap to rotate the cutterhead until the lock screws securing one of the knives are accessible between the tables. Cover the edge of the knife with a rag to protect your hands, then use a wrench to loosen each screw *(above)*. Lift the knife and the retaining wedge out of the cutterhead.

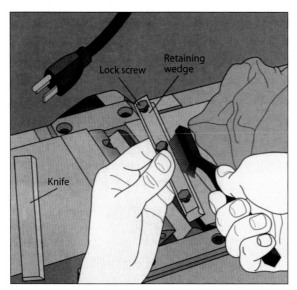

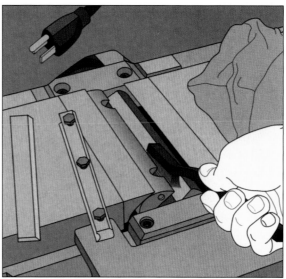

Cleaning the retaining wedge

Clean any pitch or gum from the retaining wedge using a brass-bristled brush dipped in solvent *(above, left)*. If the face of the retaining wedge that butts against the knife is pitted or rough, you may have trouble setting the knife height when reinstalling the knife. Flatten the face of the wedge as you would the sole of a plane *(page 40)* until it is smooth. Also use the brush to clean the slot in the cutterhead that houses the retaining wedge and knife *(above, right)*.

Installing the knife in a sharpening jig

Use a commercial knife-sharpening jig to sharpen the jointer knife. Center the knife in the jig bevel up and clamp it in place by tightening the wing nuts; use a rag to protect your hand *(right)*. Make sure that the blade is parallel with the lip of the jig. If the knife does not extend out far enough from the jig, insert a wood shim between the knife and the jig clamps.

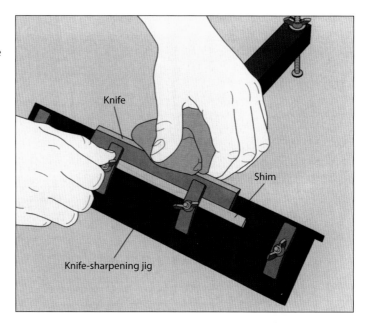

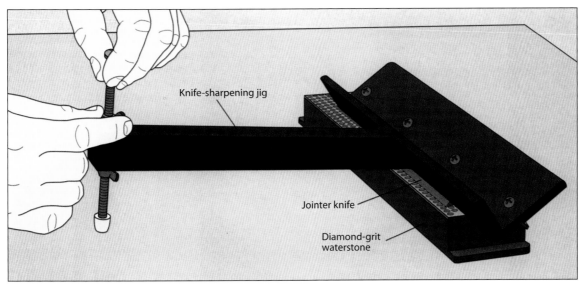

Knife-sharpening jig

Jointer knife

Diamond-grit
waterstone

Sharpening the knife

Set a sharpening stone on a flat, smooth work surface; in the illustrations on this page, a diamond-grit waterstone is shown. To adjust the jig so the beveled edge of the jointer knife is flat on the stone, turn the jig over, rest the bevel on the stone, and turn the wing nuts at the other end of the jig *(above)*. Lubricate the stone—in this case with water—and slide the knife back and forth. Holding the knob-end of the jig flat on the work surface and pressing the knife on the stone, move the jig in a figure-eight pattern *(below)*. Continue until the bevel is flat and sharp. Carefully remove the knife from the jig and hone the flat side of the knife to remove any burr formed in the sharpening process.

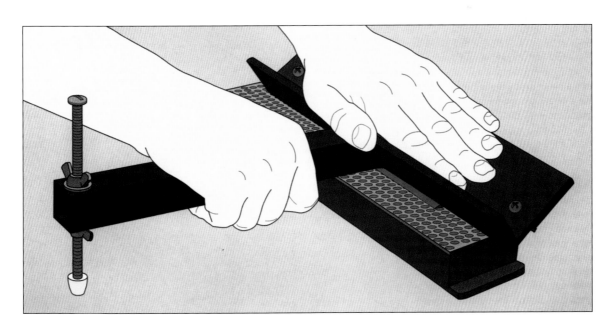

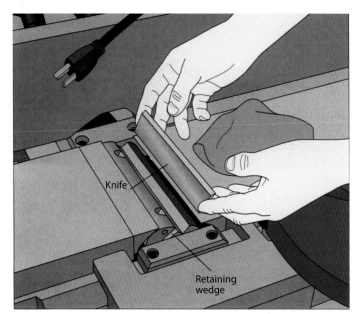

Knife

Retaining
wedge

Reinstalling the knife in the jointer

Insert the retaining wedge in the cutterhead,
centering it in the slot with its grooved edge
facing up. With the beveled edge of the knife
facing the outfeed table, slip it between
the retaining wedge and the front edge
of the slot, leaving the bevel protruding
from the cutterhead.

Setting the knife height

Adjust the height of the knife using a
commercial jig *(page 85)*, or do the job by hand,
as shown at right. Cover the edge of the knife
with a rag and partially tighten each lock screw
on the retaining wedge. Use a small wooden
wedge to rotate the cutterhead until the edge
of the knife is at its highest point—also known
as Top Dead Center or TDC. Then, holding the
cutterhead stationary with a wedge, place a
straight hardwood board on the outfeed table
so that it extends over the cutterhead. The knife
should just brush against the board along the
knife's entire length. If not, use a hex wrench to
adjust the knife jack screws. Once the knife is at
the correct height, tighten the lock screws on
the retaining wedge fully, beginning with the
one in the center and working out toward the
edges. Sharpen and install the remaining knives
the same way.

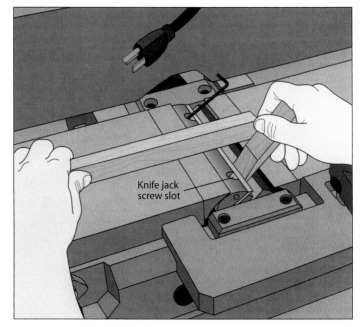

Knife jack
screw slot

Installing Jointer Knives with a Jig

Using a knife-setting jig

The jig shown at right features magnetic arms that will hold a jointer knife at the correct height while you tighten the retaining wedge lock screws. Insert the knife in the cutterhead and position it at its highest point as you would to install the knife by hand *(page 84)*. Then mark a line on the fence directly above the cutting edge. Position the knife-setting jig on the out-feed table, aligning the reference line on the jig arm with the marked line on the fence, as shown. Mark another line on the fence directly above the second reference line on the jig arm. Remove the jig and extend this line across the outfeed table. (The line will help you quickly position the jig the next time you install a knife.) Reposition the jig on the table, aligning its reference lines with the marked lines on the fence. Then use a wrench to tighten the lock screws *(right)*.

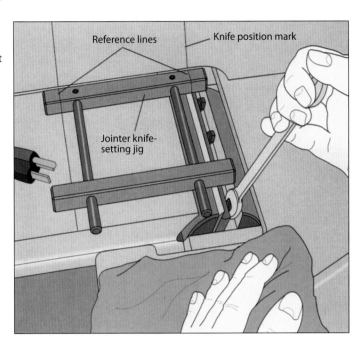

Reference lines — Knife position mark

Jointer knife-setting jig

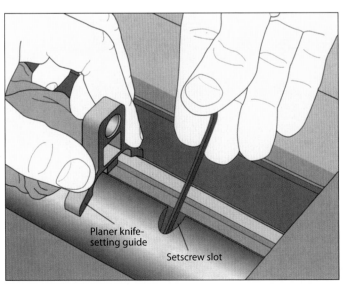

Planer knife-setting guide

Setscrew slot

Sharpening Planer Knives

Removing and installing a planer knife

Remove a planer knife from the machine and sharpen it as you would a jointer knife *(page 81)*. To reinstall the knife use the knife-setting guide supplied with the machine or a commercially available model like the one shown on page 79. Place the knife in the planer cutterhead and partially tighten the setscrews. Hold the knife-setting guide beside one of the set-screws so that its two feet are resting on the cutterhead on each side of the opening. Then adjust the setscrew with a hex wrench until the edge of the knife contacts the bottom of the guide *(left)*. Repeat for the remaining setscrews.

Sharpening Blades and Bits — Back to **Basics**

Carving Tools

Good carving is achieved only by using properly sharpened tools. The highest-quality chisel, knife, or gouge will produce inferior results without proper sharpening. This section demonstrates the sharpening skills and tools you need to practice the craft.

The sharpening tools and accessories that you use should be chosen with care. Using a carborundum grinding stone, for example, can damage your chisel because it will overheat the cutting edge, rendering it too soft to cut properly. The high speed of most stationary grinders adds to this problem. The solution is to use rubber grinding wheels containing tiny fragments of industrial diamonds, and to buy or build a slow-speed grinder.

To test the sharpness of the cutting edge of your tool after following the sharpening instructions in this chapter, make a cut on the end of a piece of scrap wood. Working across the grain, the blade should slice evenly through the wood, producing a curl of waste wood and leaving behind a smooth surface. Also note the sound that the blade produces: A razor-sharp carving tool will make a clean, hissing sound as it slices through the wood.

Common Sharpening Do's and Don'ts

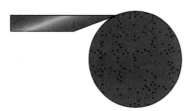

Too much on the edge
This will create a double bevel that will not cut properly.

Too much on the heel
This will produce a concave bevel that will cause the chisel to gouge into the wood.

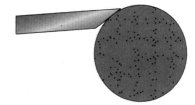

Proper angle
This produces a flat bevel, with the correct angle of between 15° and 35°.

Uneven bevel
Makes the chisel difficult to control and produces uneven cuts; caused by sharpening the bevel in some areas more than others.

Slanted gouge or V-tool
The cutting edge is angled forward instead of being perpendicular to the shaft, as is desirable.

Hook on a V-tool
This point of excess metal forms at the apex of the V during the initial sharpening; it must be ground away.

Sharpening Tools and Accessories

Stationary grinder
Aluminum oxide wheel turns too fast for most sharpening, but is useful for truing badly nicked carving tools.

Cotton polishing wheel
Used in place of a strop to polish and hone cutting edges.

Polishing compound
Abrasive dabbed in small quantities on cotton wheels for polishing.

Rubber grinding wheel
The best type of grinding wheel for carving tools; tiny bits of diamond are embedded in the wheel, providing the abrasive necessary for sharpening.

Strop
Polishes the edge of a tool after it has been ground.

Bench stone
Any oilstone or water-stone used to sharpen carving tools.

Auger file
Used for sharpening small, hard-to-reach cutting edges.

Diamond hones
More durable than traditional bench stones.

Wheel dresser
Used periodically to true the surface of a grinding wheel.

Honing cone
Used for sharpening gouges.

Carving Tools

Back to **Basics**

87

Sharpening a Knife

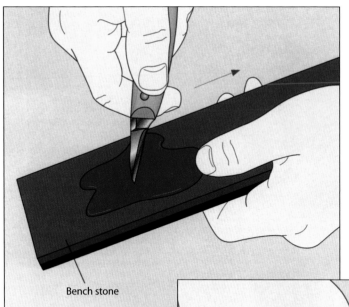

Bench stone

Honing the cutting edge

Apply the appropriate lubricant to your sharpening stone, then hold the blade of the knife at a 15 to 35 degree angle. A lower angle is more suitable if you are working with softwood; a higher angle will work better with hardwood. Slice toward yourself as if you were trying to slice a piece from the stone, making sure you keep your other hand well clear of the cutting edge *(left)*. Then make a cut in the opposite direction. Continue, alternating the direction of your slicing.

Stropping the knife

Sharpening will create tiny burrs on the cutting edge that can be removed with a leather strop. Holding the strop in one hand, draw the blade across the strop away from the cutting edge *(right)*. (Stropping into the edge will cause the knife to cut the strop.) Repeat the process on both sides of the blade.

Strop

Sharpening a Chisel on a Grinder

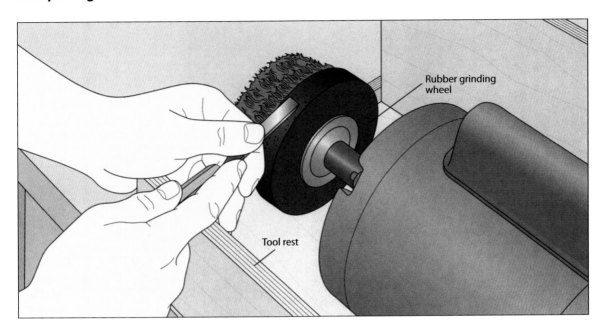

Rubber grinding wheel

Tool rest

Honing the cutting edge

Install a rubber grinding wheel and a cloth wheel on a bench grinder. Holding the blade between the index finger and thumb of one hand, set the handle on the tool rest and start grinding at the heel of the bevel. A thin edge of reflected light will be visible at the tip of the blade *(above)*. Draw the chisel down the grinding wheel until the extreme end of the cutting edge touches the grinding wheel. At this point, the thin line of the reflection will disappear. The final bevel should vary between 15 and 35 degrees, with a steeper angle required for cutting hardwoods. A skew chisel is sharpened the same way *(left)*, except that you need to perform the process on both sides of the blade since it has a bevel on each face *(inset)*.

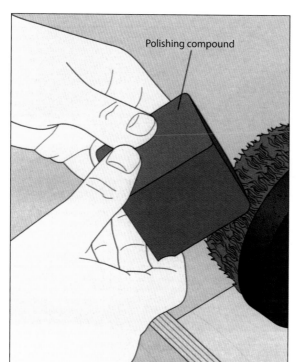

Polishing compound

Buffing the chisel

Apply some polishing compound to the cloth wheel on your grinder while it is spinning. Then hold one side of the chisel edge against the wheel *(top, right)*. Flip the chisel over and polish the opposite side. This will remove any small burrs left by the honing process.

Shop Tip

A sharpening-stone holder

Carvers must sharpen their tools frequently. To make the process more convenient, build a permanent home for your stone. Outline the sharpening surface on a piece of solid wood large enough to be clamped to your bench. Then plow a recess within the outline using a router fitted with a straight bit; make the depth of the recess slightly more than one-half the thickness of the stone. Square the corners of the recess with a chisel and store the stone in the holder. When you need to sharpen, simply secure the board to your workbench.

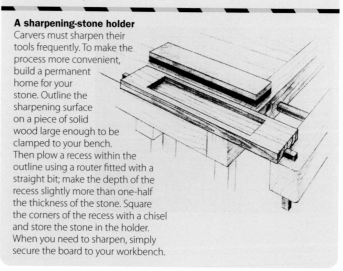

A Bench Grinding Station

This shop built grinding station rotates the wheel so the grinding surface turns away from the operator, contrary to the rotation of a standard bench grinder. This is better for carving tools as it allows a lighter touch of the blade against the grinding wheel to hone the cutting edge, which in turn prevents overheating the tool. This station also permits you to reduce the wheel's speed simply by increasing the size of the pulley on the arbor.

Bolt a ¼-horsepower motor to the rear of your work surface. The surface should be at least an inch thick—preferably two inches—and stand 30 to 36 inches off the floor, depending on your height and the level at which you like to work. Mount a small pulley on the motor. Use a commercial arbor to mount the grinding wheels. The arbor should be bolted so its pulley is in line with the motor pulley. The pulley on the arbor should be sized to reduce the revolutions of the motor to between 800 and 1,100 rpm on the grinder. So, if the motor rotates at 1,750 rpm, you will need roughly half that speed for the grinding wheels. Therefore, the diameter of the pulley on the arbor should be twice that of the pulley on the motor.

A V-belt transfers power from the motor to the arbor. Make sure the arbor is positioned so the belt is taut and you have a space four inches wide in front of the grinding wheel to mount a tool rest. (Some arbors come equipped with their own tool rest.)

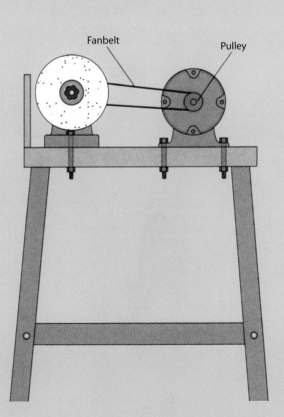

Fanbelt
Pulley

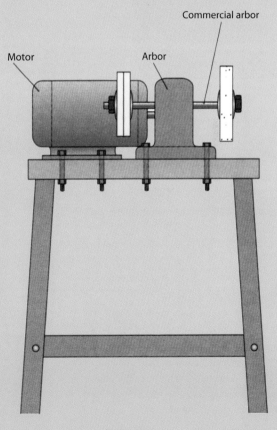

Commercial arbor
Motor
Arbor

Sharpening a Chisel on a Bench Stone

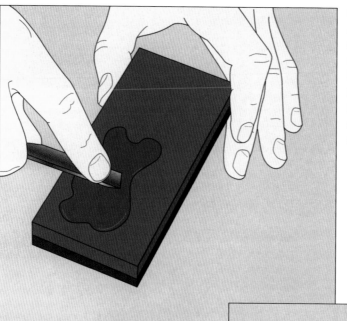

Grinding the edge

Apply the appropriate lubricant to the bench stone, then place it on a work surface. Grasp the stone with one hand. With the other hand, hold the blade with the bevel flat on the stone. Rub the cutting edge in a circular motion *(left)*. Do not rock the chisel or hold it at too steep an angle or you will end up forming a double bevel on the blade.

Polishing the cutting edge

Use a leather strop or the buffing wheel of a bench grinder to polish both sides of the blade. If you are using a strop, hold it in one hand, while drawing the edge of the chisel toward you *(right)*. Draw both the top and bottom across the strop several times, to remove any tiny burrs, and the bevel is polished to a fine edge.

Sharpening a V-Tool

Grinding the edges

Treat the cutting edge as if it were two separate flat chisels *(see page 89)*. Start grinding at the rear of the heel of the bevel. A thin line of light will appear at the tip of the blade. Slowly draw the chisel down the wheel until the tip of the cutting edge touches the wheel. The reflected light should disappear.

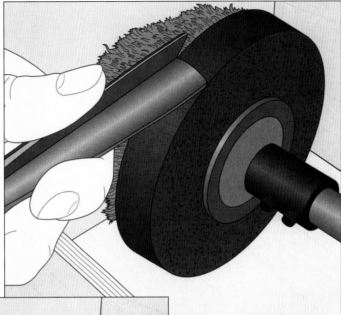

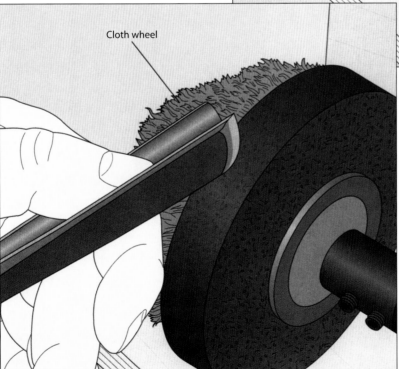

Cloth wheel

Removing the point

After grinding the two edges of the V-tool, a slight hook will form where the edges meet. Remove this point by resting the V-tool on the grinding wheel, with the hook just touching the wheel. Rock the tool gently from side to side until the point is removed *(left)*. Then buff both sides of the cutting edge on a cloth wheel.

Gouge-Grinding Jig

The jig shown at right allows you to hold a gouge at the correct angle for grinding. The dimensions will accommodate most gouges. Cut the base and guide from ½-inch plywood. Screw the guide together and fasten it to the base with countersunk screws. Make the guide opening large enough for the arm to slide through freely.

Cut the arm from 1-by-2 stock and the tool support from ½-inch plywood. Screw the two parts of the tool support together, then fasten the bottom to the arm flush with one end. For the V-block, cut a small block to size and saw a 90° wedge out of one side. Glue the piece to the tool support.

To use the jig, secure it so the arm lines up directly under the grinding wheel. Seat the gouge handle in the

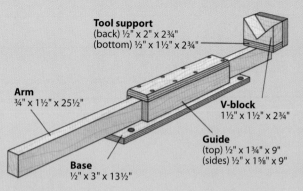

Tool support
(back) ½" x 2" x 2¾"
(bottom) ½" x 1½" x 2¾"

Arm
¾" x 1½" x 25½"

V-block
1½" x 1½" x 2¾"

Guide
(top) ½" x 1¾" x 9"
(sides) ½" x 1⅝" x 9"

Base
½" x 3" x 13½"

V-block and slide the arm so the beveled edge of the gouge sits flat on the grinding wheel. Clamp the arm in place. Then, with the gouge clear of the wheel, switch on the grinder and reposition the tool in the jig. Roll the beveled edge across the wheel *(below)*.

Sharpening a Gouge

Honing the cutting edge

Holding the blade between the fingers and thumb of one hand, set the heel of the bevel on the wheel. Roll the gouge from side to side, grinding as evenly as possible. Slowly draw back the gouge, sliding it down the surface of the grinding wheel as you continue a sideways rolling motion. A thin line of reflected light at the extreme edge of the gouge will be visible until you begin grinding the extreme edge. This sliver of light will disappear, indicating you have reached the edge *(right)*. Do not slide the gouge any further, or you will create a double bevel. Make certain that the edge is perpendicular to the shaft—it should not jut forward, nor recede beyond the corners of the cutting edge. These corners should be pointed, not rounded.

Corners

Polishing the cutting edge

Polish the cutting edge of the gouge with a cotton wheel *(left)*. You can buff the inside face, but do not attempt to grind it. Grinding could change the geometry of the gouge and reduces the carving ability of the tool.

Sharpening Techniques

Carving tools are supplied in various degrees of sharpness. In Great Britain, blades are given a basic grind before they are sold *(photo, page 99)*, needing only to be honed and polished before use. North American manufacturers, on the other hand, supply carving tools in a wide range of conditions, from fully sharpened to crudely—and sometimes improperly—ground. The majority of new carving tools require some grinding before they can be whetted, honed, and polished to a razor-sharp edge. The two main goals of grinding are to thin the dull side of the cutting edge *(inset below)* and provide the correct bevel angle for the tool. To avoid drawing the temper as you grind the metal, a wet-wheel grinder is the best choice. If you are using a dry wheel, the tool must be cooled with water frequently.

Grind the bevel to an angle between 20° and 30° and make certain it is flat. The bevel must extend across the entire width of the blade and be square to the tool's edges. In general, a lower bevel angle will produce finer cuts, but its thin cutting edge will tend to break during use, particularly in harder woods. To strengthen the edge, hone an inside bevel with a slipstone *(page 101)*. Carvers generally try to grind the lowest bevel angle that still resists breaking. Ultimately, only experimentation and experience will teach you what angle is best for your tools and style of carving.

Grinding a Carving Tool

Grinding a gouge blade

Grind the bevel on a gouge blade using a grinder with a medium-grit wheel. Position the guard properly, adjust the tool rest to the desired bevel angle, and turn on the machine at its slowest setting. Holding the blade between the index finger and thumb of one hand, set the blade on the tool rest and advance it until the bevel is flat on the wheel. (If you wish to alter the bevel angle of the cutting edge, hold the blade against the wheel at the desired angle.) With your index finger against the tool rest, roll the blade on the wheel until the entire edge is ground *(right)*. Continue, checking the blade regularly, until the cutting edge has been thinned *(below)* and the bevel angle is correct. Dip the blade in water occasionally to prevent it from overheating. Use the same technique for chisels and V-parting tools, but move the blade from side to side straight across the wheel.

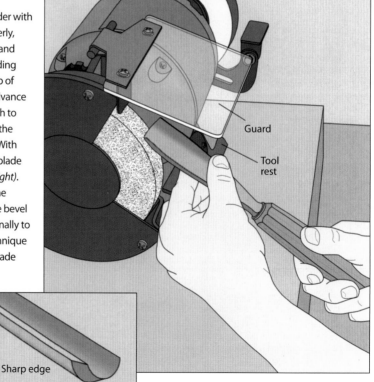

Guard

Tool
rest

Dull edge   Sharp edge

Courtesy Veritas Tools 1990

Sharp tools are essential for carving wood. Not only will they improve the quality of your work, they will also make it more enjoyable. Once you have ground the proper bevel on your tool *(page 96)*, you will need to hone and polish the blade before it is ready for work.

For carving chisels, both sides of the blade must be whetted, or honed, on a benchstone, and polished on a strop as shown at right and on page 98. The procedures for gouges and V-parting tools are a little more involved. In both cases, the outside bevel must be whetted. Depending on the quality of the bevel you produced on the blade, you may first have to use a medium stone and then move to a fine stone to achieve the desired sharpness. If the bevel has been properly ground, a fine stone should suffice.

The whetting process will raise a burr on the inside edge of the blade, which is honed away with a slipstone. This second process creates a slight inside bevel on the blade that strengthens the cutting edge. The angle of the inside bevel can be anywhere from 5° to 10°. Once the inside bevel is honed, the outside edge may need to be honed to a final edge with a slipstone. If the edge is sufficiently keen, however, both the inside and outside bevels are simply polished with a strop or the buffing wheel of a bench grinder. The steps for sharpening a V-parting tool are shown on page 100; for a gouge, see page 102.

Sharpening a Carving Chisel

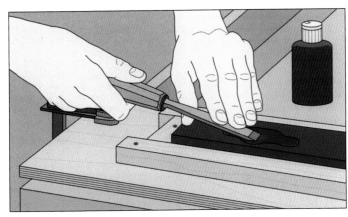

Honing the cutting edge
Lay a combination medium/fine stone on a plywood base, screw cleats alongside the stone to keep it from moving, and clamp the base to a work surface. Lubricate the stone with a few drops of light machine oil until it pools on the surface. Start by holding the blade with the outside bevel flat on the stone and slide the cutting edge back and forth until the rough grinding marks have disappeared *(above)* and a burr has formed on the inside edge. Flip the tool and repeat the procedure to hone the inside bevel. Both bevels should be about 20°.

Back to *Basics*

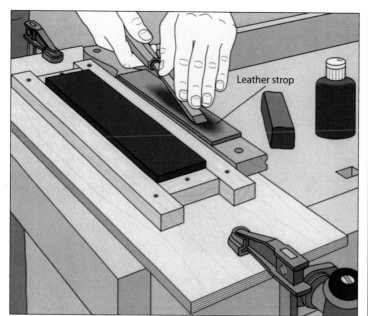

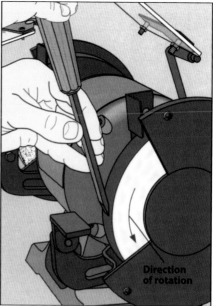

Leather strop

Direction
of rotation

Polishing the cutting edge

Use a leather strop or the buffing wheel of a bench grinder
to polish both sides of the blade. If you are using a strop, you
can fasten it to the base alongside the sharpening stone.
Apply a light coating of polishing compound to the strop,
hold the chisel with the outside edge on the leather, and
draw the chisel toward you in long strokes, keeping the bevel
flat *(above, left)*. Lift the tool at the end of each stroke. To
polish a blade with the buffing wheel, hold the chisel almost
vertically, with the bevel flat against the buffing wheel
(above, right). Move the chisel from side to side slowly as the
wheel polishes the bevel. Whether you are using the strop
or the wheel, continue until the burr remaining from the
honing process disappears and the bevel is polished to a fine
edge. Repeat on the other side of the blade.

Most carving tools require some grinding before they can be honed and polished to a razor-sharp edge. The British-made tools shown at right (from left to right, a chisel, a skew chisel, a gouge, and a V-tool) have been ground properly and are ready for final sharpening. The edges are fairly sharp with none of the dullness shown in the inset on the previous page. The bevels are flat and square to the edges of the tool.

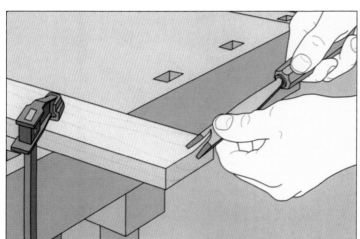

Testing for sharpness

There is no guarantee that the first sharpening of the blade will produce the keen edge required for carving. When you have honed and polished the blade, clamp a piece of pine or another softwood to the work surface and cut across the grain of the board. The blade should shear the wood cleanly without tearing out the fibers. Also note the sound that the blade produces; a razor-sharp carving tool will make a clean, hissing sound as it slices through the wood.

Carving Tools

Back to *Basics*

Sharpening a V-Tool

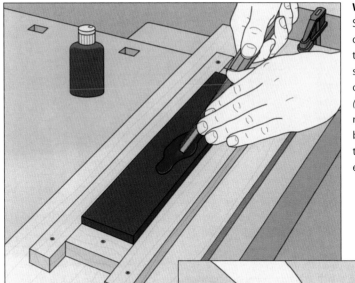

Whetting the outside edges

Sharpen each side of a V-tool separately. Hone one outside bevel as you would a chisel, moving the blade back and forth along the length of a saturated oilstone and keeping the bevel flat on the stone. Repeat on the other side of the V *(left)*. Stop working when you have removed the rough marks from the ground edge and a small burr forms on the inside of the edge. To feel for the burr, run your finger gently across the inside edge of the blade.

Removing the hook

When you sharpen the outside bevels of a V-tool, a hook of excess metal will form at the apex of the V *(inset)*. This hook must be ground away before you hone the inside bevel. Holding the tool on the stone, roll the corner across the surface *(right)*. Move the tool from end to end along the stone until you wear away the hook and an outside bevel forms at the apex of the V. As much as possible, try to blend the bevel with the outside bevels on the sides of the V, forming one continuous beveled edge. This process will create a burr in the center of the inside edge, which will be removed.

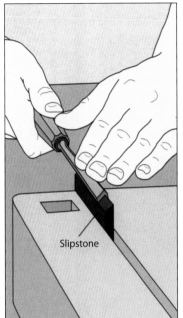

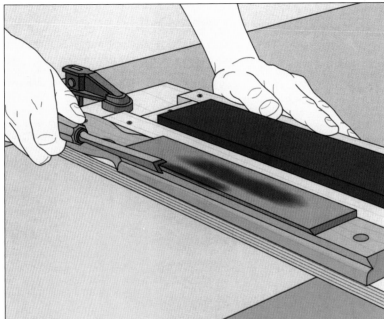

Slipstone

Shop Tip

**Slipstones
and strops for
inside edges**
The inside edges of
carving tools—
particularly
gouges and
V-tools—can be
difficult to hone and
strop, if you do not have a
slip-stone or strop of the correct
shape. You can fashion a substitute for
honing a gouge by wrapping a dowel
with 600-grit sandpaper *(near right).* For
V tools, attach the paper to a piece of scrap
wood with an outside edge shaped like the inside
angle of the blade. Use glue to secure the sandpaper
in place. Contoured strops can be improvised by
fastening a strip of leather to a suitably shaped wood
block. A simpler option is to fold a strip of leather to fit the
inside edge of the gouge or V-tool *(far right).*

Honing the inside bevel
To remove the burr and hone an inside bevel,
use a triangular slipstone that matches the
angle of the V-tool blade as closely as possible.
Clamp the stone securely in a bench vise and
saturate it with oil. To avoid crushing the stone,
do not overtighten the vise. Then, with only
the end of the blade's inside edge in contact
with the stone, draw the tool forward and back
applying light downward pressure *(above, left).*
Check the inside edge of the blade periodically
until the burr is removed and a slight inside
bevel forms. To finish, polish the outside of the
edge with a leather strop or a bench grinder
polishing wheel *(page 98).* To polish the inside
edge, cut the side of a commercial strop to
match the interior angle of the V-tool and draw
the tool along the angled edge *(above, right).*

Sharpening a Gouge

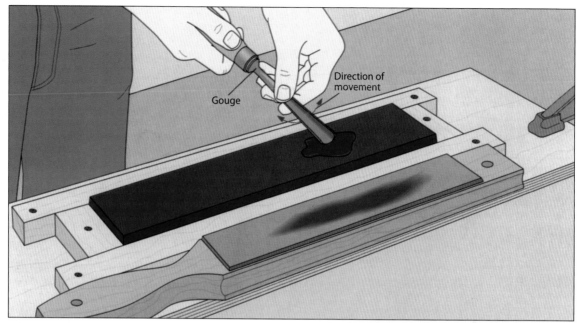

Whetting the outside bevel

Saturate an oilstone as you would to sharpen a chisel *(page 92)*, then set the outside bevel of the gouge flat on the stone. Starting at one end, move the blade back and forth along the stone with a rhythmic motion, simultaneously rolling the tool so the entire bevel contacts the sharpening surface *(above)*. Avoid rocking the blade too far, as this will tend to round over its corners and blunt the cutting edge. Continue until the bevel is smooth and a burr forms on the inside edge of the blade. The same technique is used to sharpen a front-bent, or spoon gouge, but you will need to hold the tool at a much higher angle to keep the bevel flat on the stone *(right)*.

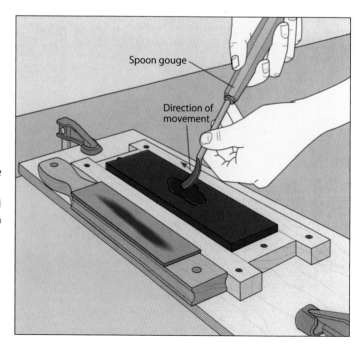

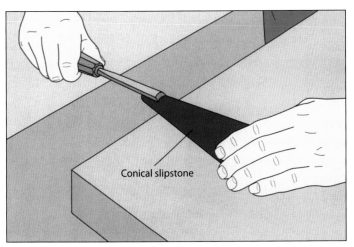

Conical slipstone

Honing an inside bevel

Once you have sharpened the gouge blade's outside bevel, use a conical slip-stone to hone a slight inside bevel on the blade and remove the burr. Put a few drops of oil on the cutting edge of the gouge, then move the blade away from you across the stone. To avoid dulling the outside edges of the blade—and bringing the cutting edge close to your fingers—the blade should only contact the narrow portion of the stone *(left)*. Continue until the burr is removed and an inside bevel of 5° to 10° forms.

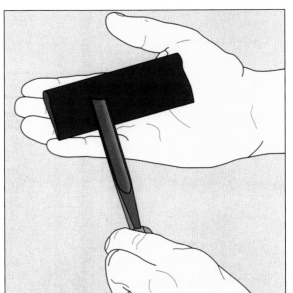

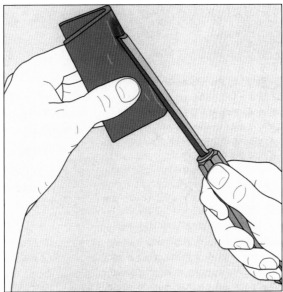

Refining the outside bevel

Use a fine slipstone to refine the gouge's outside bevel and remove any burr that may have formed during sharpening. Apply a few drops of oil to the cutting edge, then hold the slipstone in one hand and set the bevel flat on its surface. Draw the tool from side to side along the stone, rotating the blade to hone the bevel *(above)*. To protect your hand, work only in the middle portion of the stone. Continue honing until the burr is worn away.

Polishing the inside bevel

Use a folded piece of leather to strop the inside bevel of the gouge. Spread some polishing compound on the leather and fold it so its edge matches the inside curve of the gouge. Draw the blade along the leather repeatedly to polish the inside bevel *(above)*. You can also do the polishing using a shaped wood scrap *(page 104)*.

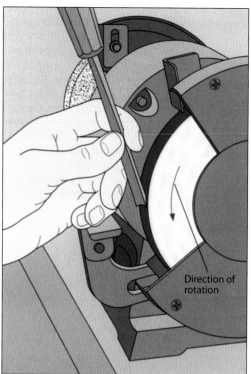

Direction of rotation

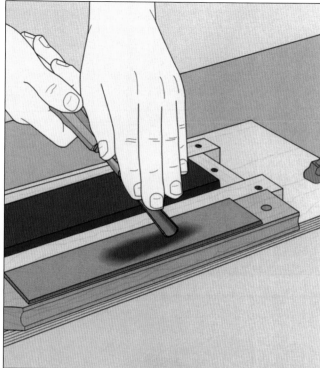

Polishing the outside bevel

Use a felt wheel on a grinder or a leather strop to polish the outside bevel of the gouge. To use a wheel, move the tool rest out of the way, turn on the tool, and hold a stick of polishing compound against it for a few seconds. Then, holding the gouge handle firmly in your right hand, pinch the blade with the fingers of your left hand and set the bevel flat against the wheel. Making sure the blade only contacts the lower half of the wheel, lightly roll the tool across the wheel to polish the bevel *(above, left)*. If you use a strop, spread some polishing compound on it, then use the same rolling technique shown before to polish the outside bevel *(above, right)*. Check the inside bevel; if a burr has formed, repolish.

Shop Tip

Using wood scraps for stropping

Instead of a leather strop or a buffing wheel, you can use shaped wood scraps to strop the cutting edges of your carving tools. Cut a groove in one board that matches the convex, edge of a gouge *(near right)*; cut the reverse shape for the concave edge of the blade *(far right)*. You can use the gouge itself to perfect the shape of the scraps. To use a wooden strop, spread some polishing compound on the contoured surface and draw the cutting edge along the wood.

Grinding Wheel Identification

Choosing a grinding wheel

The wheels supplied on grinders are usually too coarse for use with turning tools. A wide variety of replacement stones are available, but selecting the right one is no simple matter. You need to decipher the codes marked on the side of the wheels, describing their composition and abrasive quality. The chart below will help you interpret these codes. (They are usually found sandwiched between two numerical manufacturer's symbols on the side of the stone.) If you plan to use a wheel to grind carbon steel tools, and then hone with a benchstone, buy a wheel marked A 80 H 8 V. This means the wheel is aluminum oxide (A), fine grained (80), and relatively soft (H), with a medium structure or concentration of abrasives (8). The particles are bonded together by a process of heat and fusion, known as vitrification (V). For high-speed steel tools, a medium hardness of I or J is better. If you plan to use your tools right off the grinder, choose a wheel with a grain size of 100 or 120.

Standard Marking System Chart			
Abrasive Type	**A**: Aluminum oxide	**C**: Silicon carbide	**Z**: Aluminum zirconium
Abrasive (Grain) Size	**Coarse**: 8, 10, 12, 14,16, 20, 24	**Medium**: 30, 36, 46, 54, 60	**Fine**: 70, 80, 90, 100, 120, 150, 180 **Very fine**: 220, 240, 280, 320, 400, 500, 600
Grade Scale	**Soft** **Medium** **Hard** A B C D E F G H I J K L M N O P Q R S T U V W X Y Z		
Structure	**Dense** ⟶ **Open** 1 2 3 4 5 6 7 8 9 10 11 12 13 14 15 16 etc		
Bond	**B**: Resinoid **BF**: Resinoid reinforced **E**: Shellac **O**: Oxychloride **R**: Rubber		
Type	**RF**: Rubber reinforced **S**: Silicate **V**: Vitrified		

Courtesy of the American National Standards Institute

Grinding Turning Tools

The angle at which you present a tool to the grinder will determine the angle of the bevel. The diagram at right shows the angles at which gouges, scrapers, and skew chisels should be held to the grinding wheel to produce suitable bevels.

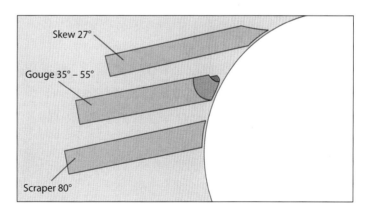

Skew 27°
Gouge 35° – 55°
Scraper 80°

Dressing a Grinding Wheel

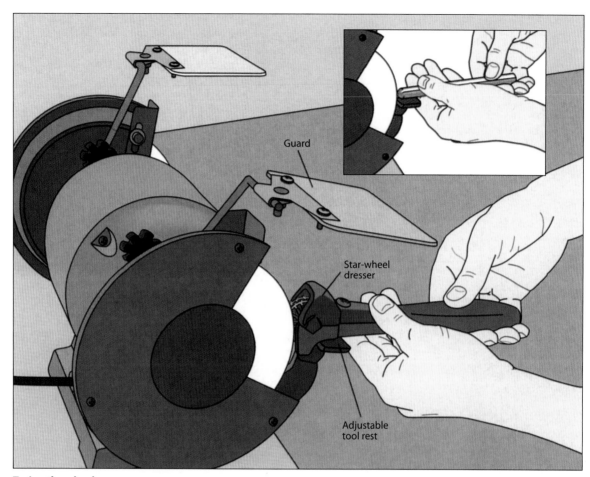

Guard

Star-wheel dresser

Adjustable tool rest

Truing the wheel

A grinding wheel should be trued when ridges or hollows appear on the stone or it becomes discolored. You can use either a star-wheel or a diamond-point dresser. For the star-wheel dresser shown at left, move the grinder's tool rest away from the wheel. With the guard in position, switch on the grinder and butt the tip of the dresser against the wheel.

Then, with your index finger resting against the tool rest, move the dresser from side to side. To use the diamond-point dresser *(inset)*, hold the device between the index finger and thumb of one hand, set it on the tool rest, and advance it toward the wheel until your index finger contacts the tool rest. Slide the tip of the dresser across the wheel, pressing lightly while keeping your finger on the tool rest. For either dresser, continue until the edges of the wheel are square and you have exposed fresh abrasive.

Turning Tool Tips

Carving Tools

Back to **Basics**

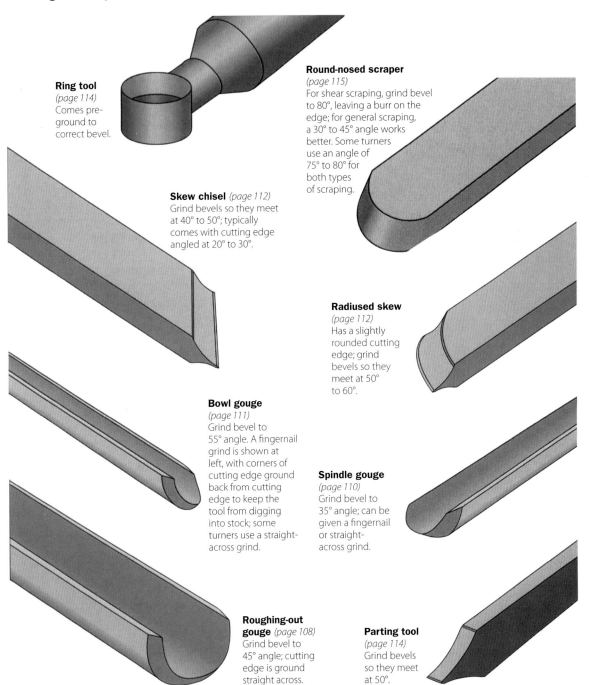

Ring tool
(page 114)
Comes pre-ground to correct bevel.

Round-nosed scraper
(page 115)
For shear scraping, grind bevel to 80°, leaving a burr on the edge; for general scraping, a 30° to 45° angle works better. Some turners use an angle of 75° to 80° for both types of scraping.

Skew chisel *(page 112)*
Grind bevels so they meet at 40° to 50°; typically comes with cutting edge angled at 20° to 30°.

Radiused skew
(page 112)
Has a slightly rounded cutting edge; grind bevels so they meet at 50° to 60°.

Bowl gouge
(page 111)
Grind bevel to 55° angle. A fingernail grind is shown at left, with corners of cutting edge ground back from cutting edge to keep the tool from digging into stock; some turners use a straight-across grind.

Spindle gouge
(page 110)
Grind bevel to 35° angle; can be given a fingernail or straight-across grind.

Roughing-out gouge *(page 108)*
Grind bevel to 45° angle; cutting edge is ground straight across.

Parting tool
(page 114)
Grind bevels so they meet at 50°.

Sharpening a Roughing-Out Gouge

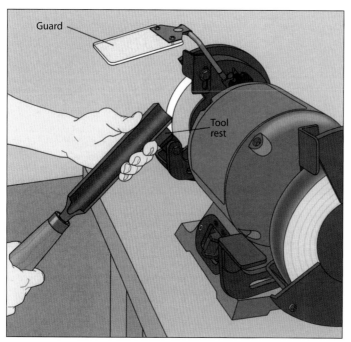

Guard

Tool
rest

Restoring the bevel

Position the guard and turn on the machine. Holding the blade between the fingers and thumb of one hand, set the cutting edge on the tool rest and advance it until the bevel lightly contacts the grinding wheel. If you want to change the bevel angle of the cutting edge, adjust the tool rest to the desired angle. With your index finger against the tool rest, roll the blade on the wheel until the entire edge is ground, keeping the bevel flat on the wheel at all times. Continue, checking the blade regularly, until the cutting edge is sharp and the bevel angle is correct. To prevent the blade from overheating, occasionally dip it in water if it is carbon steel, or remove it from the wheel to let it cool if it is high-speed steel. If your grinder has a felt or cloth wheel, use it to polish the cutting edge. Otherwise, use a slipstone.

Polishing the cutting edge

Move the tool rest out of the way, turn on the grinder, and hold a stick of polishing compound against the felt wheel for a few seconds to impregnate it with abrasive. Then, with the gouge almost vertical, grip the handle in your right hand, hold the blade between the fingers and thumb of your left hand, and set the bevel flat against the wheel. Lightly roll the blade from side to side across the wheel to polish the bevel. A slight burr will form on the inside edge of the tool. To remove it, roll the inside face of the blade against the wheel until the burr rubs off. Test the tool for sharpness by cutting a wood scrap across the grain. The blade should slice easily through the wood.

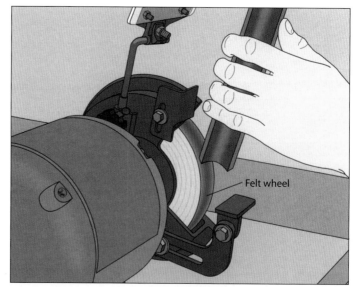

Felt wheel

Gouge-Sharpening Jig

The jig shown below guarantees that the tips of longer and larger gouges will contact your grinding wheel at the correct angle to restore the bevel on the cutting edge. The dimensions given in the illustration below will accommodate most turning gouges.

Cut the base and guide from ½-inch plywood. Screw the guide together and fasten it to the base with screws countersunk from underneath. Make sure the opening created by the guide is large enough to allow the arm to slide snugly but freely.

Cut the arm from 1-by-2 stock and the tool support from ½-inch plywood. Screw the two parts of the tool support together, then fasten the bottom to the arm, flush with one end. For the V block, cut a small wood block to size and saw a 90° wedge out of one side. Glue the block to the support.

To use the jig, secure it to a work surface so the arm lines up directly under the grinding wheel. Seat the gouge handle in the V block and slide the arm so the beveled edge of the gouge lies flat on the grinding wheel. Clamp the arm in place. Then, with the gouge clear of the wheel, switch on the grinder and reposition the tool in the jig. Holding the gouge with both hands, rotate the beveled edge across the wheel (below). Stop occasionally to cool the blade and check the cutting edge periodically until you are satisfied with the results.

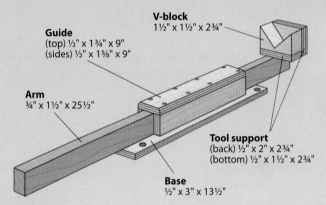

V-block
1½" x 1½" x 2¾"

Guide
(top) ½" x 1¾" x 9"
(sides) ½" x 1⅝" x 9"

Arm
¾" x 1½" x 25½"

Tool support
(back) ½" x 2" x 2¾"
(bottom) ½" x 1½" x 2¾"

Base
½" x 3" x 13½"

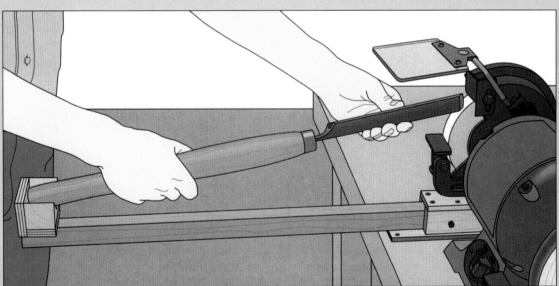

Sharpening a Spindle Gouge

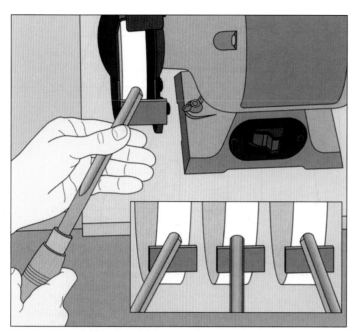

Sharpening on a bench grinder

Position the guard properly and turn on the grinder. Pinching the blade between the fingers and thumb of one hand, set the blade flat on the tool rest and advance it until the bevel lightly contacts the stone *(left)*. Adjust the tool rest, if desired, to change the bevel angle. If the tool has a square grind, roll the bevel on the stone as you would for a roughing-out gouge *(page 108)*. If the tool has a fingernail-grind, roll the cutting edge on the wheel and pivot the handle from left to right while keeping the bevel flat on the grinding wheel at all times *(inset)*. Continue rolling the blade and moving the tool handle from side to side until the edge is sharpened, stopping occasionally to check the grind and cool the tip.

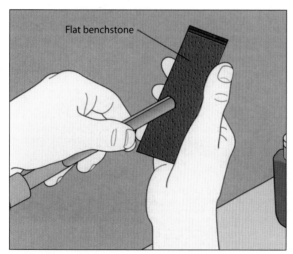

Flat benchstone —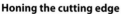

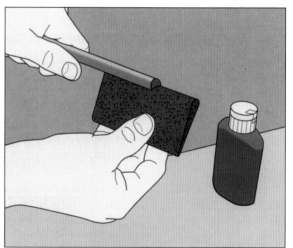

Honing the cutting edge

Once the bevel has been sharpened on the grinder, use a flat benchstone to polish the tool to a razor-sharp edge. Saturate the stone with oil, then roll the outside bevel across the abrasive surface *(above, left)* to create two microbevels on the cutting edge. Use a convex slipstone matching the curvature of the gouge to remove the burr that forms on the inside of the cutting edge. Put a few drops of oil on the slipstone and hone the inside edge until the burr rubs off *(above, right)*.

Sharpening a Bowl Gouge

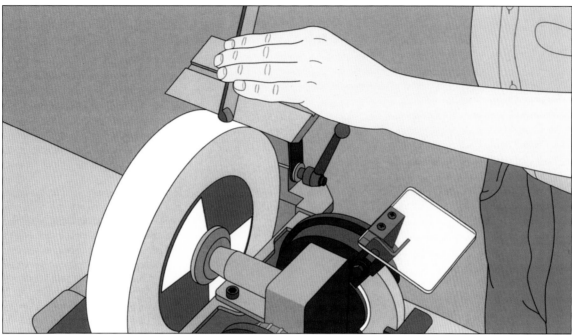

Shop Tip

Sharpening with a belt sander

If you do not own a bench grinder, you can grind your turning tools on a belt sander. Install a 100-grit belt, mount the tool upside down in a stand, and clamp the stand to a work surface. To grind a turning tool, turn on the sander and press the bevel flat on the belt.

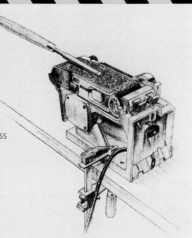

Using a wet/dry grinder

Adjust the tool rest so the bevel will rest flush with the wheel surface, then turn on the grinder. Hold the gouge flat on the tool rest and advance the tool until the bevel is flat on the stone. Then, holding the blade in place, roll the edge across the stone *(above)*, pivoting the handle as necessary to keep the bevel flat on the wheel at all times. Continue until the tool is sharp. The gouge is now ready to use.

Sharpening a Skew Chisel

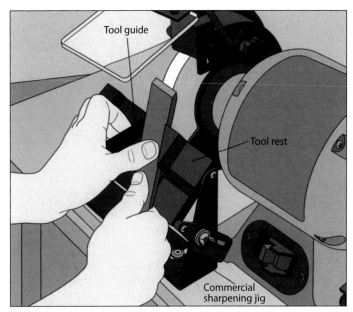

Tool guide

Tool rest

Commercial
sharpening jig

Using a jig
Position a commercial sharpening jig in front of the grinding wheel as close to the wheel as possible without touching it. Set up the jig following the manufacturer's instructions. On the model shown, you can adjust the tool table to the correct angle for any tool—in this case, a straight skew chisel. Place the tool guide supplied with the jig in the groove in the rest and hold the chisel in the guide. Butt one edge of the chisel blade against one side of the groove in the guide so the cutting edge is square to the grinding wheel. Turn on the grinder and advance the tool until the bevel contacts the wheel. Slide the tool guide from side to side to sharpen the bevel. Flip the tool over and repeat the process with the tool against the other edge of the groove in the guide *(left)*. When both bevels are sharpened, hone a microbevel. The same techniques can be used without benefit of a sharpening jig, using the grinder's tool rest.

Sharpening a Radiused Skew Chisel

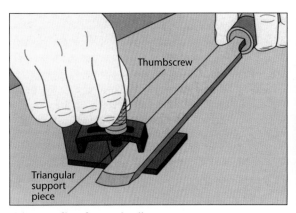

Thumbscrew

Triangular
support
piece

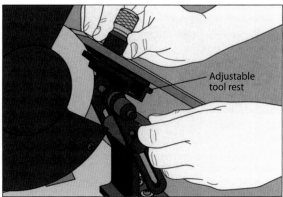

Adjustable
tool rest

Using a radius sharpening jig
Secure the chisel in a commercial jig specially designed for sharpening radiused skew chisels. For the model shown, hold the long edge of the chisel blade against the triangular support piece in the center of the jig and tighten the thumbscrew so that the bevel will lie flat on the grinding wheel when you sharpen it *(above, left)*. Now, position an adjustable tool rest in front of the grinding wheel and set the jig on it, ensuring that the pivot pin on the bottom of the jig slides in the hole in the center of the tool rest. Adjust the angle of the rest so the bevel sits flat on the wheel, then tighten it in position *(above, right)*. Turn on the grinder and pivot the bevel across the wheel, keeping the jig pressed down on the tool rest at all times.

Sharpening the second bevel

Once the first bevel is sharpened, turn off the grinder and wrap a piece of masking tape around the chisel blade where it meets the bottom edge of the jig. This will enable you to turn the chisel over and reposition it in the jig so that the second bevel you grind is identical to the first. Remove the chisel from the jig, turn it over, and reposition it so the bottom edge of the jig is aligned with the tape. Turn on the grinder and sharpen the second bevel *(right)* the same way you ground the first.

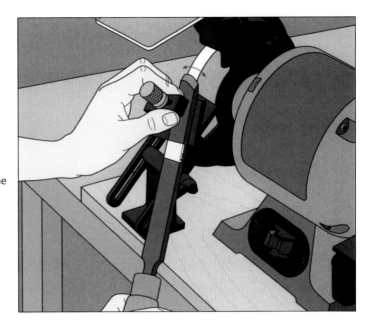

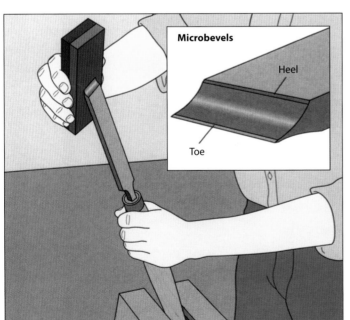

Microbevels

Heel

Toe

Creating microbevels

The grinding process will create a rough hollow-ground, or concave, bevel on the tool blade. The heel and toe of the bevel of either straight or radiused blades must be honed to a smooth cutting edge before the chisel is used. To support the chisel, wedge its handle in the lathe bed, then put a few drops of oil on the fine side of a combination stone. Rub the stone across the bevel *(left)*, creating microbevels on both the heel and toe of the bevel *(inset)*. Repeat the procedure on the other side of the tool. As the tool becomes dull with use, you do not need to regrind it. Simply restore the microbevels. After several honings, however, the microbevels will disappear and the bevel will flatten out. At this point, you will have to regrind the tool to restore the hollow-ground bevel.

113

Sharpening a Parting Tool

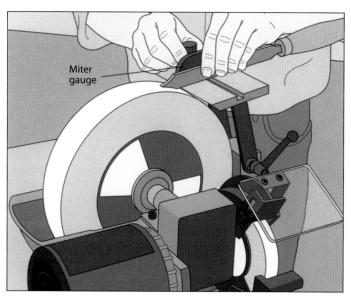

Miter gauge

Using a wet/dry grinder

Adjust the tool rest so the bevel on the parting tool will lie flat on the wheel. Hold the blade on edge on the tool rest with one side against the miter gauge supplied with the rest, then turn on the grinder and advance the tool until the bevel contacts the wheel. Pressing the tool lightly against the grinder, slide the gauge back and forth until the bevel is sharpened. Repeat the process to sharpen the bevel on the other side *(left)*. Once both bevels are the same and the cutting edge is sharp, hone microbevels as you would on a skew chisel *(page 113)*.

Sharpening a Ring Tool

Using a commercial jig

Some ring tools come with a jig for holding the tip during sharpening and a conical stone for honing the inside edge. Follow the manufacturer's instructions to sharpen your ring tool. For the model shown at right, install the sharpening stone in the collet of a router and clamp the tool upside down on a work surface. Detach the tip from the handle of the ring tool and install it in the jig. Turn on the router and press the tip lightly against the spinning stone to sharpen the edge. When the first side is sharp, flip the tool and hone the other side of the ring.

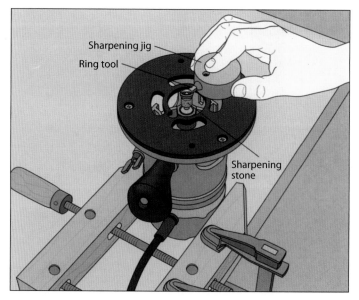

Sharpening jig
Ring tool
Sharpening stone

Sharpening a Scraper

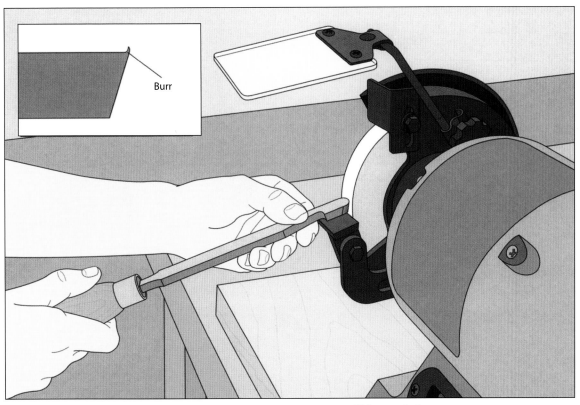

Burr

Shop Tip

Burnishing a scraper
Wet grinders do not leave enough of a burr on scraper blades; you can produce a more even burr by burnishing the edge. Using firm, even pressure, draw a burnisher across the end of the blade to raise a burr on its top edge.

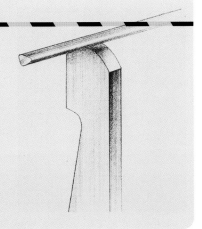

Using a grinder
Position the guard properly and adjust the tool rest so the bevel on the end of the scraper will rest flush against the wheel. Turn on the grinder and hold the blade between the fingers and thumb of one hand. With the blade flat on the tool rest, advance the tool until the bevel lightly contacts the wheel. Pass the entire edge across the wheel *(above)*, moving the handle from side to side. Stop occasionally and run your finger lightly over the end of the tool to feel for a burr *(inset)*. Stop sharpening when an even burr has formed.

Index

A

adzes, 51, 53
aluminum oxide wheels, 16
angle checker, 17
angle jig, 17
Arkansas oilstones, 8, 14, 15, 18
auger bit files, 17
auger bits, 55, 56–57
auger files, 87

B

band saw blades, 60, 73–78
 cleaning, 73
 folding and storing, 78
 heat-resistant guide blocks for, 58, 75
 installing and setting, 74
 repairing (soldering), 76–77
 rounding, 75
 sharpening, 73–75
belt sander, sharpening with, 42, 111
bench grinders
 components, illustrated, 21
 dressing grinding wheel, 22, 106
 grinding station, 91
 illustrated, 16, 21
 mobile sharpening dolly, 23
 specifications and functions, 20
 step-by-step sharpening process, 15
 truing wheels, 106
 wheels for, 16, 20, 21, 22, 87, 105–6
bench planes
 anatomy of, illustrated, 39
 assembling and adjusting, 45
 checking sole for square, 41
 disassembling and cleaning, 40
 honing end of cap iron, 44
 lapping sole of, 41
 refurbishing, 40–41
 sharpening, 41–44
 testing for sharpness, 44
benchstones, 18–19. See also slipstones
 holders for, 17, 23, 90
 honing microbevel on, 43
 illustrated, 16, 87
 oilstones, 18
 polishing bevel on, 49
 sharpening
  chisels, 32, 92
  gouges, 35–38, 102–4
  jointer/planer knives, 81–83
  knives, 88
  spokeshaves, drawknives, inshaves, adzes, 52–53
  V-tools, 38, 100–101
 smoothing cutting edge with, 14
 step-by-step sharpening process, 15
 truing (flattening), 19
 waterstones, 18, 19

bevels and microbevels
 creating hollow-ground bevel, 42
 honing microbevels, 15, 43
 illustrated, 15
 for individual tools. See specific tools and categories of tools
 sharpening do's and don'ts, 86
bit files, 17
bits and shapers
 about
  overview of, 58
 auger bits, 55, 56–57
 for braces, 55–57
 brad-point bits, 68–69
 drill bit grinding attachment, 58–59, 61
 drill bits, 60, 65–69
 drill bit-sharpening jig, 61, 66
 Forstner bits, 67–68
 gallery of, 60
 router bit sharpener, 61
 router bits and shaper cutters, 60, 62–63
 sharpening
  auger bits, 56–57
  brad-point bits, 68–69
  Forstner bits, 67–68
  router bits, 62–63
  spade bits, 69
  spoon bits, 57
  twist bits, 58–59, 65–66
 spade bits, 69
 spoon bits, 55, 57
 storage rack for shaper cutters, 63
 twist bits, 58–59, 65–66
blades and knives. See also band saw blades; hand tools
 about
  overview of, 58
 circular saw blades, 60, 70–72
 circular saw blade-setting jig, 61, 72
 circular saw blade-sharpening jig, 61, 72
 drawknives, 24–25, 51, 53
 gallery of, 60
 jointer and planer knives, 60, 79–85
 jointer/planer-knife sharpening jig, 61, 79
 knife-setting jigs, 61, 79
 molding knives, 60, 64
 sharpening
  band saw blades, 73
  circular saw blades, 72
  drawknives, 24–25, 53
  jointer and planer knives, 79–83, 85
  knives, 88
  molding knives, 64
book overview, 6–7
bowl gouges, 107, 111
braces and bits, 55–57
brad-point bits, 68–69
burnishers, 46
burnishing, 47–48, 49, 50, 115
burnishing angle, maintaining, 50

burrs
 creating, 15, 34, 36, 38, 46, 88, 97, 100
 removing, 15, 24, 34, 35, 36, 38, 43, 47, 53, 54, 98, 101

C

cabinet scrapers, 46, 48–50
cant-saw files, 17
carving tools. See gouges and chisels; turning tools
ceramic stones, 19
chisels. See gouges and chisels
circular saw blades, 70–72
 blade-setting jig, 61, 72
 blade-sharpening jig, 61, 72
 changing, 70–71
 cleaning, 71
 illustrated, 60
 sharpening, 72
commercial resin solvent, 60, 71
cutting edge
 defined, 14
 smoothing, 14

D

diamond needle files, 17
diamond stones, 19, 44
diamond-coated honing files, 17, 87
diamond-point dressers, 16, 22, 106
dolly, for mobile sharpening, 23
drawknives, 24–25, 51, 53
dressers, 16, 87
dressing grinding wheels, 22, 106
drill bit grinding attachment, 58–59, 61
drill bits, 60, 65–69
drill bit-sharpening jig, 61, 66

F

felt wheels, 16
files, 17
Forstner bits, 67–68

G

gouge slipstone, 19
gouges and chisels, 30–38. See also turning tools
 replacing handles, 31
 sharpening, 89–104
  carving gouges, 33–38, 100–104
  chisels, 32, 86, 89–90, 92, 97–99
  do's and don'ts, 86
  grinding carving tools and, 96–97
  grinding station for, 91
  roughing-out gouges, 33–34
  spindle gouges, 35
  tools and accessories for, 33, 87, 94
  V-tools, 38, 86, 93, 100–101
 shop-made jig for cleaning/removing burrs, 24
 turning tools, 105
 types of, illustrated, 30
gouge-sharpening jig, 33, 94, 109

grinders. *See* bench grinders; wet/dry grinders
grinding station, 91
grinding step, 15

H
hand scrapers, 46, 47–48
hand tools, 24–57. *See also* bench planes; gouges and chisels
  about
    sharpening, 24
    advantages of, 24
    adzes, 51, 53
    braces and bits, 55–57
    choosing durable ax handles, 54
    drawknives, 24–25, 51, 53
    handsaws, 26–29
    hewing hatchets, 51
    inshaves, 51, 53
    roughing and shaping tools, 51–54
    scrapers, 46–50
    spokeshaves, 51, 52, 54
handles
  durable, for axes, 54
  replacing on chisels and gouges, 31
handsaws, 26–29
hewing hatchets, 51
honing compound, 16
honing cones, 87
honing guides, 17, 34, 60
honing step, 15

I
inshaves, 51, 53
inside-edge strops, 101

J
Japanese waterstones, 8, 15, 18, 19
jointer and planer knives, 60, 79–85
  cleaning, 79
  honing jointer knives, 79–80
  installing/adjusting jointer knives, 84–85
  sharpening jointer knives, 81–83
  sharpening planer knives, 85
jointer/planer-knife sharpening jig and knife-setting jig, 61, 79

K
knife honing guide, 60
knife-setting jigs, 61, 79
knives. *See* blades and knives

L
lapping compounds, 17, 19
lapping step, 15, 40, 43
lapping table, 19, 23

M
mobile sharpening dolly, 23
molding knives, 60, 64
multi-tool jigs, 16

N
neoprene polishing wheels, 16

O
oilstones
  truing (flattening), 19
  types and characteristics, 18
overheating, 10

P
parting tools, 107, 114
planer knives. *See* blades and knives
planes. *See* bench planes
polishing compound, 87, 90
polishing step, 15
polishing wheels, 16, 87

R
radiused skew chisels, 107, 112–13
resin solvent, 60, 71
ring tools, 107, 114
roughing and shaping tools, 51–54
roughing-out gouges, 33–34, 107, 108–9
round-nosed scrapers, 107, 115
router bit sharpener, 61
router bits and shaper cutters, 60, 62–63
rust removers, 34

S
sander, sharpening with, 42, 111
saw holders, 27, 28
scrapers, 46–50
  burnishers and, 46, 115
  cabinet, 46, 48–50
  hand, 46, 47–48
  round-nosed, turning tool, 107, 115
  types of, illustrated, 46
shapers. *See* bits and shapers
sharpening. *See also specific tools and categories of tools*
  about
    overview of basics, 12
  bevels and. *See* bevels and microbevels
  blades. *See* blades and knives
  cutting edge and, 14
  do's and don'ts, 86
  grinders for. *See* bench grinders
  with sander, 42
  step-by-step process, 15
  stones. *See* benchstones
  tools and accessories for, 16–17, 61, 86–87
single-cut bastard mill files, 17
skew chisels, 30, 107, 112
slipstones, 19, 35, 36, 38, 53, 64, 101, 103, 110
spade bits, 69
spindle gouges, 35, 107, 110
spokeshaves, 51, 52, 54
spoon bits, 55, 57
Starr, Richard, 8–9
stropping, 34, 88, 104
strops, 17, 87, 101

T
table saw blades
  changing, 70
  sharpening, 72
three-square files, 17
"tip burning," avoiding, 10
truing (flattening) benchstones, 19
turning tools, 105–15
  grinding, 105
  sharpening
    bowl gouges, 111
    parting tools, 114
    radiused skew chisels, 112–13
    ring tools, 114
    roughing-out gouges, 108–9
    scrapers, 115
    skew chisels, 112
    spindle gouges, 110
    tools and accessories for, 87
  types of, illustrated, 107
twist bits, 58–59, 65–66

V
value of sharp tools, 8
V-tools, 38, 86, 93, 100–101

W
waterstones
  storage unit, 17
  truing (flattening), 19
  types and characteristics, illustrated, 19
Waymark, Ian, 10–11
wet/dry grinders
  advantage of, 51
  components, illustrated, 21
  illustrated, 16, 21
  sharpening bowl gouge on, 111
  sharpening parting tool on, 114
wheel dressers, 20, 22, 87, 106

Index

Back to **Basics**

117

THE *Missing* SHOP MANUAL SERIES

These are the manuals that should have come with your new woodworking tools. In addition to explaining the basics of safety and set-up, each *Missing Shop Manual* covers everything your new tool was designed to do on its own and with the help of jigs & fixtures. No fluff, just straight tool information at your fingertips.

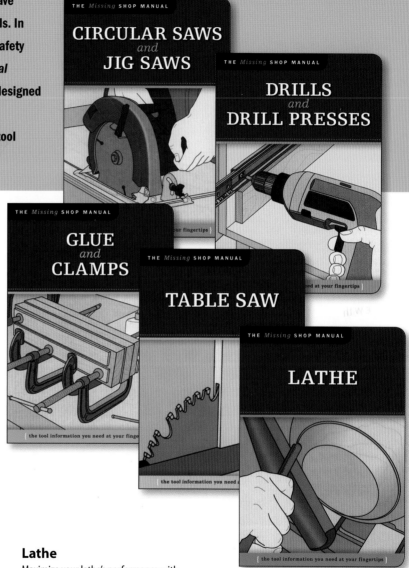

Circular Saws and Jig Saws
From ripping wood to circle cutting, you'll discover the techniques to maximize your saw's performance.

ISBN 978-1-56523-469-7
$9.95 USD • 88 Pages

Drills and Drill Presses
Expert tips and techniques on everything from drilling basic holes and driving screws to joinery and mortising.

ISBN 978-1-56523-472-7
$9.95 USD • 104 Pages

Glue and Clamps
Learn how to get the most out of your clamps and that bottle of glue when you're carving, drilling, and building furniture.

ISBN 978-1-56523-468-0
$9.95 USD • 104 Pages

Table Saw
Whether you're using a bench top, contractor or cabinet saw, get tips on everything from cutting dados and molding to creating jigs.

ISBN 978-1-56523-471-0
$12.95 USD • 144 Pages

Lathe
Maximize your lathe's performance with techniques for everything from sharpening your tools to faceplate, bowl, and spindle turning.

ISBN 978-1-56523-470-3
$12.95 USD • 152 Pages

BUILT to LAST

Discover the timeless woodworking projects that are *Built to Last*. These are the classic and enduring woodworking projects that stand the test of time in form and function and in the techniques they employ. Ideal for all skill levels, the *Built to Last* series represents the pieces and projects that every woodworker should build in a lifetime.

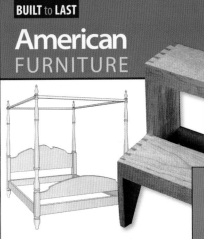

Shaker Furniture
Delve into this old-world style with 12 enduring projects. Includes step-by-step instruction and crisp drawings of each project.
ISBN 978-1-56523-467-3
$19.95 USD • 144 Pages

American Furniture
These classic furniture projects are the reason many people get into woodworking. Build your skills and confidence as you build beautiful furniture.
ISBN 978-1-56523-501-4
$19.95 USD • 136 Pages

Outdoor Furniture
12 practical projects to furnish your outdoor living space. Organized, step-by-step instruction will help you build smart and get it done right.
ISBN 978-1-56523-500-7
$19.95 USD • 144 Pages

Look for These Books at Your Local Bookstore or Woodworking Retailer

Get *Back to Basics* with the core information you need to succeed. This new series offers a clear road map of fundamental woodworking knowledge on sixteen essential topics. It explains what's important to know now and what can be left for later. Best of all, it's presented in the plain-spoken language you'd hear from a trusted friend or relative. The world's already complicated—your woodworking information shouldn't be.

Woodworker's Guide to Joinery

ISBN 978-1-56523-462-8
$19.95 USD • 200 Pages

Constructing Kitchen Cabinets

ISBN 978-1-56523-466-6
$19.95 USD • 144 Pages

Woodworking Machines

ISBN 978-1-56523-465-9
$19.95 USD • 192 Pages

Setting Up Your Workshop

ISBN 978-1-56523-463-5
$19.95 USD • 152 Pages

Woodworker's Guide to Carving

ISBN 978-1-56523-497-0
$19.95 USD • 160 Pages

Woodworker's Guide to Wood

ISBN 978-1-56523-464-2
$19.95 USD • 160 Pages

Look for These Books at Your Local Bookstore or Woodworking Retailer